D1058973

Cambridge Papers in Sociology   No. 2

WORKERS' ATTITUDES AND TECHNOLOGY

Workers' Attitudes
and Technology

by DOROTHY WEDDERBURN
Reader in Industrial Sociology
Imperial College, University of London

and ROSEMARY CROMPTON
Lecturer in Sociology
University of East Anglia

CAMBRIDGE
AT THE UNIVERSITY PRESS
1972

301.55
W38 w

Published by the Syndics of the Cambridge University Press

Bentley House, 200 Euston Road, London, NW1 2DB

American Branch: 32 East 57th Street, New York, N.Y. 10022

© Cambridge University Press 1972

Library of Congress Catalogue Card Number: 70-183225

ISBNs: 0   521   07432   0   hard covers
          0   521   09711   8   paperback

Printed in Great Britain by Alden & Mowbray Ltd.
at the Alden Press, Oxford

HD
6331
.W38

CONTENTS

JUL 25 '74

HUNT LIBRARY
CARNEGIE-MELLON UNIVERSITY

List of Tables

Acknowledgements

This study was financed by a grant from the Social Science Research Council and administered by the Department of Applied Economics, Cambridge University, and we are grateful to both of these bodies. The Company, which wishes to remain anonymous, gave every assistance and we wish that we could thank by name the many people who gave so generously of their time. The shop stewards, too, overcame their initial suspicions and helped us freely and we would like to thank them most warmly. As is always the case with studies based on field work, we owe a special debt to the men who cooperated in the interviews and talked so enthusiastically and willingly to us. We could not have carried out the study without our loyal interviewing team, which included: Kathleen Carter, Helen Forman, Peter Hobbs, Constance Oliver, Bridget Rees, and Olwen Smith.

Christine Craig supervised the interviewing and was also largely responsible for the coding and analysis of that part of the study. Alex Easterbrook also gave considerable help with the analysis and Bill Lampton generously wrote a programme which enabled us to analyse the material on the Imperial College computer. There have been a number of typed versions of the monograph and Christine Dawson of Imperial College and Diane Watkins of the Massachusetts Institute of Technology have been the willing victims of our many changes of mind.

John Goldthorpe, Celia Davies, R. M. Blackburn, A. Stewart and J. Mortimer have made helpful comments on various drafts, but are not, of course, implicated by anything we say.

Finally, we would like to record our great debt to Joan Woodward who sadly did not live to see the final outcome of the work in which she took so much interest.

HUNT LIBRARY
CARNEGIE-MELLON UNIVERSITY

1 Technology and the Study of Organisations

This monograph has been written as a contribution to the current debate among industrial sociologists about the place of technology as an explanatory variable in the study of attitudes and behaviour within organisations. To understand the shape which the report takes it should be seen in a general setting. The authors share the besetting sin of so many academics of taking too long to prepare their material for publication. Our survey data was collected at the end of 1965. The first reports were written in 1966. Subsequent field work was carried out in 1967 and 1968. Now, four years later, we have benefited from reading the results of new studies in this field, of which there have been a number, as well as from the ongoing discussions we have had with our colleagues at Imperial College.[1] Our original interpretation of the data has not changed fundamentally. But its re-examination in the light of new research findings stimulated us to ask new questions. Sometimes our resources were inadequate and the questions have had to remain unanswered. But sometimes we were fortunate enough to be able to reanalyse our material and to collect additional information. The account presented here, therefore, is in one sense the story of the unfolding and development of a research project.

It began with a survey embarked upon for purposes which appear rather far removed from questions about the influence of technology upon structure and behaviour in organisations. It was part of an investigation into the nature and extent of differences in the terms and conditions of employment of manual and non-manual workers and of attitudes towards those differences.[2]

---

1 For a summary of the Imperial College work see ed. J. Woodward, *Industrial Organisation: Behaviour and Control*, Oxford University Press, 1970. For a contribution adopting a very different approach see J. H. Goldthorpe, D. Lockwood, F. Bechhofer, J. Platt, *The Affluent Worker: Industrial Attitudes and Behaviour* Cambridge University Press, 1968., and *The Affluent Worker in the Class Structure*, Cambridge University Press, 1969.
2 See D. Wedderburn "The Conditions of Employment of Manual and Non-Manual Workers" in *Social Stratification and Industrial Relations*, ed. John Goldthorpe and Michael Mann, S.S.R.C., Cambridge, 1969, mimeographed; and D. Wedderburn and J. C. Craig, *"Relative Deprivation in Work"* paper read to Section N of the British Association for the Advancement of Science, Exeter, September, 1969.

In so far as conditions of employment—that is such things as fringe benefits—of manual workers were becoming more like those of non-manual workers, it might be hypothesised that this would occur first in the most advanced technological conditions where the most highly skilled manual workers would be employed. Thus the influence of technology was seen as of some, but certainly not of prime, importance, in the research design of that particular study. Among other things, however, we carried out a large-scale attitude survey of a sample of manual workers in the employment of one major company, on a site where a number of different technologies were in use. Some marked differences of attitude were revealed between groups employed in different works where the production systems were also very different.

This finding was not altogether unexpected for a considerable body of literature was already available to suggest an association between technology and workers' attitudes and behaviour. For example, in the fifties, the workers at the Tavistock Institute developed the concept of an open socio-technical system". This was derived from the:

> "consideration that any production system requires both a techno-logical organisation—equipment and process layout—and a work organisation relating to each other those who carry out the necessary tasks. The technological demands place limits on the type of work organisation possible, but a work organisation has social and psycho-logical properties of its own that are independent of technology. . ." [1]

At the same time the analysis pointed

> "in particular to the various ways in which enterprises are enabled by their structural and functional characteristics ('system constants') to cope with the 'lacks' and gluts in their available environment." [2]

There was an emphasis upon the constraints imposed by the hardware of the production system upon the social system. In other words, the kind of social relationships which would develop in the work situation would be shaped and limited by things like the kind of machinery in use, its layout and the sequencing of production tasks. However, it was argued that there was no

---

1 A. K. Rice, *Productivity and Social Organisation*, Tavistock Publications, London, 1958. p.4.
2 F. E. Emery and E. L. Trist, "Socio-Technical Systems" in ed. C. W. Churchman and M. Verhulst, *Management Science, Models and Techniques,* Vol. 2., Pergamon Press, Oxford, 1960, p.94.

one-to-one relation between the requirements of the technological and the social systems:

"but what is logically referred to as a correlative relation." [1]

This made possible an emphasis upon the uniqueness of the constellation of social and psychological aspects of each individual work organisation.

Concurrently Joan Woodward had been examining the assumptions of classical management theory which implied that there were certain general principles of organisation which had a universal validity and that the adoption of 'correct' organizational principles would lead to 'success'. As a result of her South East Essex studies she had concluded that this was not the case. She did, however, find that firms using

"similar technical methods had similar organisation structures." [2]

Differences of technology seemed to be associated with different management structures. A further conclusion was that technology also affected human relations in the plant:

"there appear to be considerable differences between production systems in the extent to which the 'situational demands' create conditions conducive to human happiness." [3]

or, as it was more fully argued:

"Some factors—the relaxation of pressure, the smaller working groups, the increasing ratio of supervisors to operators, and the reduced need for labour economy—were conducive to industrial peace in process production. Thus, although some managements handled their labour problems more skilfully than others, these problems were much more difficult for firms using the middle ranges (i.e. batch production) than those in unit or process production." [4]

Joan Woodward was concerned to develop a 'middle-range' theory of organisation. She believed that her studies supported the view that structure

---

1 Ibid., page 87.
2 Joan Woodward, *Management and Technology*, H.M.S.O., London, 1958, p.16.
3 Ibid., p.30.
4 Ibid., p.18.

was dependent upon the type of technology in use. If technology, as the independent variable could be conceptualised in a way which would enable it to be measured then it would be possible to test this hypothesis. She therefore made one of the first systematic attempts to classify technology for purposes of sociological analysis. She combined the engineering characteristics of the production process (unit, batch, mass and continuous) with the nature of the product (integral or dimensional) to produce eleven categories of technology.[1]

Meanwhile, in the Unites States, Blauner had drawn attention to what he has termed the preoccupation of industrial sociologists with the situation of the assembly-line worker.[2] These researches were concerned with a specific type of technology, which was the assembly line method of mass production. Blauner's own study of alienation became available just as the first stage of the present inquiry was being planned. Here was yet another sociologist laying stress upon the importance of technology in shaping workers' attitudes. Blauner examined four kinds of technology, chemical process, textile, printing and, once again, the automobile assembly line. He argued that what he called 'structural differentiation' within modern industry has led to a situation where:

> "the industrial system distributes alienation unevenly among its blue-collar labour force, just as our economic system distributes income unevenly".[3]

The most important differentiating factor which gave an industry its distinctive character was technology:

> "Technology refers to the complex of physical objects and technical operations (both manual and machine) regularly employed in turning out the goods and services produced by an industry." [4]

Therefore, it was the differences in technology which largely accounted for differences in the degree of alienation among the work force. As an example of Blauner's argument we may quote what he has to say about continuous-process industries:

---

1 Joan Woodward, *Industrial Organisation: Theory and Practice,* London, Oxford University Press, 1965, p.39.
2 R. Blauner, *Alienation and Freedom*, The University of Chicago Press, Chicago, 1964, p.5.
3 Ibid., p.5
4 Ibid., p.6.

"The case of the continuous-process industries, particularly the chemical industry, shows that automation increases the worker's control over his work process and checks the further division of labour and the growth of large factories. The result is meaningful work in a more cohesive, integrated industrial climate. The alienation curve begins to decline from its previous height as employees in automated industries gain a new dignity from responsibility and a sense of individual function."[1]

Earlier Sayles[2] and Kuhn[3] had postulated a connection between technological factors and one particular aspect of industrial behaviour, namely grievance activity. These authors saw the impact of technology as mediated through its influence upon the formation of work groups in bargaining situations.

"The ability of work groups to conduct fractional bargaining depends upon the power relationship between the work group, the union, and management, a relationship significantly influenced by the technological conditions under which a plant or industry operates."[4]

Yet despite this growing volume of literature concerned with the influence of technology, it was difficult to construct propositions about the way in which it was thought to influence attitudes and behaviour, except at a most general level. In some measure this was due to the diversity of meanings attached to the concepts 'technology', 'attitudes' and 'behaviour' by different writers. One problem for instance, was that 'technology' or 'production system' was sometimes described or classified in engineering terms and on other occasions in terms which were themselves social, that is, according to the degree of social interaction which was possible in the work situation, or according to the size of the work group. Another difficulty sprang from the fact that the various authors concerned themselves with quite different aspects of behaviour and attitudes.

---

1 Ibid., p.182.
2 L. R. Sayles, *The Behaviour of Industrial Work Groups; Prediction and Control*, John Wiley and Sons, New York, 1958.
3 J. W. Kuhn, *Bargaining in Grievance Settlement*, Columbia University Press, New York, 1961.
4 Ibid., p.144.

This is important because divergent attitudes can be expressed by the same group of workers towards different aspects of the employing organization.[1] Some studies have shown attitudes to the company and to immediate supervision which coincide, others have shown attitudes more favourable to one than to the other. Which attitudes, then, are those most influenced by technology, and what, if any, is the relationship between such attitudes and various aspects of behaviour?[2]

Just as the use of the concepts varied, so did the suggested causality. Some sociologists had laid emphasis upon the effect of technology upon the nature of the work task. Blauner, for instance, spoke of 'alienation' which dealt with the consequences of the task for the worker in terms of 'meaninglessness', feelings of 'powerlessness', isolation, 'self-estrangement'.[3]

Others, like Joan Woodward, placed more emphasis upon the nature of the control system associated with a particular technology and its consequences for workers in "the amount of discretion they have in the organization of their own activities".[4]

Furthermore, in almost all the studies referred to, comparisons of technology, however defined, were across firms and industries.[5] The broad similarity of the findings of a number of studies did suggest that other variables such as the market position of various firms, geographical location, management philosophy, degree of trade union organization, etc., were likely to be of lesser importance. Nonetheless, there was clearly interest in testing whether some of these very general associations between technology, attitudes and behaviour which had been postulated, would be repeated in a situation where some of the other variables could be held constant.

---

1 For a discussion of the different dimensions of 'involvement' in an organisation and the research task which remains if an index representing involvement in all objects of an organisation is to be constructed, see A. Etzioni, *A Comparative Analysis of Complex Organisations*, The Free Press of Glencoe, New York, p.303 et.seq.
2 For a survey of the difficulties arising from the lack of precision in the terminology and for a useful typology of behaviour see T. Kynaston Reeves "Constrained and Facilitated Behaviour—A Typology of Behaviour in Economic Organisations", *British Journal of Industrial Relations*, Vol. V., No.2., 1967.
3 Blauner, 1964, op.cit., Chapter II.
4 Woodward, 1965, op.cit., p.190.
5 For an earlier study of the attitudes of two groups in different technological settings within the same firm see W. W. Daniel "A Comparative Consideration of Two Industrial Work Groups", *Sociological Review*, Vol. 14., No.1., March, 1966.

This was the opportunity offered by the study on the Seagrass site with which the present report begins. The site contained a number of separate and distinct works using technologies which belonged to different categories in the Woodward classification.[1] But they were operating in the same geographical location against the background of a common company policy. It had been a simple matter to design the sample for the attitude survey in a way which would enable us to test for an association between workers' attitudes and technology such as would be predicted from Woodward or Blauner. When the results were first analysed they showed that certain constellations of attitudes—for example towards the interest of the job itself and towards supervision—were consistently more favourable in the continuous-flow process works and less favourable in the batch production-machine minding works. There were also important differences of attitude between tradesmen and general workers across the whole site. These findings were sufficiently striking to lead us to examine whether there were also any differences of overt behaviour between the works for instance in relation to absenteeism or willingness to engage in industrial disputes. Such differences did, indeed, exist between the works. But by this stage in the research the general debate about the influence of technology had been taken an important stage further by contributions from other sociologists.

It was, perhaps, inevitable that the emphasis upon technology in influencing behaviour, indeed in some cases attributing to it the role of the sole explanatory variable, should be challenged as being narrowly deterministic. One expression of this view put the matter in the following way:

"Thus, a currently fashionable view among industrial sociologists and some industrial relations specialists links the state or organisation of labour relations in particular industries or enterprises with their specific technologies—the argument being that a given technique of production imposes particular social relationships on its human participants and confines them within determinate 'socio-technical systems' which will produce qualities and phenomena which are not fully under their control." [2]

Turner and his colleagues had shown in this study that the state of labour relations differed considerably between different firms in the automobile industry in Britain. In particular, the level of strike activity showed great

1 See Chapter 2 for further description.
2 H. Turner, G. Clack and G. Roberts, *Labour Relations in the Motor Industry*, George Allen and Unwin, London, 1967, p.327.

variation. Yet the technology was, they argued, the same, it was mass pro-duction assembly line. Hence they questioned whether technology had any influence upon strike behaviour.

Goldthorpe emerged as another critic. In an analysis of what he called "a deviant case"—again, it is interesting to note, from the motor car industry—he argued:

> "Most previous writers, we would suggest, have tended to over-simplify the problems of workers' response to the stresses and constraints of assembly-line technology (and have tended to assume greater uniformity in this respect than tends to be the case) because they have left out of account one important *variable*: that is, the orientations which men *bring* to their employment and which *mediate between* the objective features of the work situation and workers' actual experience of, and reaction to, this situation." [1]

He argued that the starting point for explanation did not lie with the technology, which was to be seen as a limiting factor, the importance of which would vary according to the workers' perception of the situation:

> "but rather with the ordering of wants and expectations relative to work, and with the meaning thus given to work which result in men taking up and retaining assembly-line jobs." [2]

Thus prior orientations to work were to be seen as important influences upon workers' responses to any particular work situation. Wants and expect-ations, that is orientations, might also be important in influencing the way in which workers selected or decided to remain in particular jobs. When there was genuine choice of employment workers might enter jobs in a non-random fashion because they would deliberately seek work which would satisfy their particular set of needs. This process of self-selection could, in turn, result in the appearance of different constellations of attitudes and behaviour in different work settings.

Fortunately, the first stage of the Seagrass study had investigated the general attitudes to work of the sample. It had also provided information

---

1 John H. Goldthorpe, "Attitudes and Behaviour of Car Assembly Workers: A Deviant Case and a Theoretical Critique", *The British Journal of Sociology*, Vol. XVII, No.3., 1966, p.240. These arguments have sub-sequently been expanded in Goldthorpe et. al., 1968, op.cit.
2 Ibid., p.240.

about some of the social characteristics which Goldthorpe and his colleagues argued shaped orientations to work. These included factors such as how far workers had been geographically mobile and what stage they were at in their life-cycle.[1] A further analysis of the Seagrass material was clearly called for to examine whether differences in the characteristics of our sample in these respects were associated in any way with the attitudinal and behavioural differences which had been revealed.

This further analysis showed that some differences of orientation and background did exist between the general workers in the different works. As we shall argue, however, they appeared to be too small to account for the major differences of attitude to their employment situation which the survey revealed and we returned to factors in the work situation itself. But there was one group of workers at Seagrass whose expectations did stand out as being markedly different. These were the tradesmen. Compared to the general workers they were far more concerned with the nature of the work they had to do and with their status. They emphasised the importance of having control over their work and took it for granted that it should be interesting. The tradesmen displayed what could be summarised as a work 'ethos' of a general kind which seemed to be more closely linked to their identification with their craft or occupation than to the particular work situation in which they found themselves at Seagrass. The general workers, on the other hand, did not expect to find their work interesting. As we shall see, in those situations where they did find it interesting they valued their good fortune. But their first preoccupation was with pay, security and general working conditions.

If we were to make any progress with explaining the differences of attitudes and behaviour among the general workers it was clearly important to investigate in more detail. Was it possible to categorise those features of the production technology which could be described as 'constraints' for the worker? In the ongoing work in the Imperial College group a clearer distinction was being drawn between, on the one hand, the specific technology of the organisation which:

> "is then, the collection of plant, machines, tools and recipes available at a given time for the execution of the production task and the rationale underlying their utilisation. [2]

---

1 Goldthorpe 1966, op. cit., p.241.
2 ed. J. Woodward, 1970, op. cit., p.4.

and, on the other hand, the system for directing and controlling the production task. The latter formed part of the social system of the organisation but it was linked with, although not wholly determined by, the technology as defined above.

> "At any given time, the administrators and supervisors of a firm have, as one of their functions, to make the series of arrangements necessary for the achievement of the production task. It is evident that the nature of the arrangements which they make will be influenced by their current definition of the firm's production task; but in making these arrangements they will also have to take into account, among other things, the nature of the work force available at that time, and the state of the existing technology of the firm, which can be seen as a concrete cumulative residue of previous decisions about the task of the firm. The resultant arrangements for programming and control of work will form the basis for the administrative constraints which will be placed upon the individual employees." [1]

The original association found at Seagrass between attitudes and technology had been on the basis of classifying the specific technology in the most superficial way according to the hardware and recipes in use. Nothing at that time was known about similarities or differences between the works in the system for planning and controlling the production task. More field work was undertaken, therefore, to build up a picture of some aspects of this control system to see how they impinged upon the social roles of operator and first line supervisor. This involved observation in the works and further interviews with supervision and management.

At this stage the opportunity was also taken to check on some of the factors in the general environment of the different works which might have influenced such things as management worker relations, for instance, the degree of pressure being experienced in the works as a result of different degrees of market competition. We had argued that the comparison of production systems within the same company was likely to hold constant a number of factors which could easily vary considerably between companies. But we did not know how far this argument could be carried. One apparently simple point had also to be considered. Dissatisfaction both in overt behaviour and as expressed in the interviews was greatest on the works where the technology was machine minding large batch production. But this was

---

1 Ibid., p.14.

24

also the largest works. A recurrent theme in organisation theory has been the possibility that size alone is a factor of considerable importance in explaining behaviour in organisations. We therefore wanted to examine this question in relation to Seagrass.

The various stages of this inquiry are presented in the following chapters in roughly chronological order. We begin in Chapter 2 with a description of the Seagrass site, and in particular of the production technology of the three out of the five main works, which we selected for intensive study. Chapter 3 presents the basic results of the attitude survey, and compares the three works both in respect of attitudes and behaviour. It also examines the considerable differences in the position of the tradesmen and of the general workers. Concentrating for a time upon the general workers, we discuss in Chapter 4 how far grouping them by works distinguishes their differences of attitude more efficiently than grouping them by the kind of work they have to do, irrespective of which Works they belong to. In Chapter 5, still drawing upon the attitude survey material, we seek to justify our contention that the differences of background between the general workers on the three Works are so small as to be unlikely to account for their differences of attitude. But the contrast between the general workers and tradesmen emerges as considerable in a number of respects. In Chapter 6 we turn to the outcome of further field work at Seagrass where we looked at the environmental conditions of the Works. While finally, in Chapter 7, we describe the results of our study of the control systems on the three works, the kind of administrative constraints to which these control systems gave rise, and their consequences for the system of social relations between supervisor and supervised.

The general conclusion, which we argue in Chapter 8, is that the production tasks and the control systems associated with them do create situations where the actual experience of work, and of the authority relationships in which men become involved at the point of production, differ markedly. These differences are such that they can produce different responses from the workers involved. These constraints of the work situation may also lead workers to respond somewhat differently to the leadership offered to them by their trades unions. This is a single case study, but we find the evidence for such a connection very strong. However, this is not to postulate a closely determined relationship where workers have 'no control over the situation' and simply react. Rather we see it as a dynamic interaction between the needs of the workers as they feel them and as they are voiced for them by their trades unions, with, among other things, the different work situations. Certain work situations will predispose more strongly towards some responses than others over certain ranges of behaviour. We would not deny that many other variables play their part in the final development of any situation. At Seagrass differences in the market situation of the Works and management styles were among factors which could be identified as contributing to the complexities of the fabric of industrial relations on the site.

2 The Company and the Technology

A Description of the Site

Seagrass, as we have called it, is a large chemical complex in the North East of England. The region, as a whole, lacks industrial diversity,[1] and the particular area in which the site is located is dominated by two industries, steel and chemicals. Moreover, it is a heavily working class area. In 1966, seventy-two per cent of the economically active male population in the catchment area of the Seagrass site, were in manual occupations.[2] The region suffered severely in the Great Depression of the thirties and even in the post war period, at least until the middle sixties, the unemployment rate was high compared with Britain as a whole. The development of Seagrass itself had, however, helped to change this situation somewhat, and by 1965, when our study began, the company was well on its way to being a major employer of labour.

The employment situation generally was improving and there was actually a shortage of certain kinds of skilled labour. This was a region of Britain, however, where despite growing post war prosperity, fears of unemployment and its consequences remained alive. Older workers had experienced it personally in the thirties and younger workers had been raised as children in its shadow.

In 1965, Seagrass occupied a site of some 900 acres and employed about 10,000 workers. It was a post-war development which had been growing continuously over a twenty year period. The contrast between the pleasantly wooded hills which adjoined one edge of the site and the intricate, man-made patterning of pipes, distillation columns and huge cooling towers which dominated the site itself was sharp. At night it looked like fairyland with a mass of lights and flares. The working reality was another matter.

There were five main, physically separate, works on the site as well as engineering workshops, a power station and other services. All five works were chemical works in some sense, but they produced diverse commodities ranging from petro-chemicals which were the raw materials of further

---

1 For a detailed discussion of the region, see *The North East—a Programme for Regional Development and Growth*, H.M.S.O., London, Cmnd 2206. Nov. 1963.
2 *Sample Census 1966, Economic Activity County Leaflets—Yorkshire North Riding*, General Register Office, H.M.S.O., London, 1969.

processes, through to yarn and staple fibre which were the raw materials of the textile trade. The individual works were managed by separate divisions of the main company owning the site. These divisions controlled other works located elsewhere in the country, and in no case was the divisional head-quarters itself located on the Seagrass site.

The pattern of production and marketing was the responsibility of each division and in this sense it was rather as though the works on the Seagrass site belonged to separate firms. At the same time all divisions were governed by the central, overall economic policy of the company. Decisions about large-scale capital expenditure, for instance, were taken at headquarters company level. Most important, for the present discussion, employment conditions on the site were regulated by a company-wide labour policy. Responsibility for the application and coordination of this common labour policy at Seagrass rested with one of the divisions, which had a works there. This division was also responsible for the general administration of the site including the provision of common services to all the other works. So, although there were important areas where the works were following relatively independent policies, at site level, they were also operating in a common framework, sharing major resources like labour, power and transport.

These, then, were the 'laboratory conditions' in which the influence of technology upon workers attitudes and behaviour could be studied. At the beginning of the study we did not know just how complete these laboratory conditions were. For instance, we would expect managerial style to be an important element influencing general labour relations. What we could not decide without investigation was how far managerial style on the site was likely to be similar between the Works because it was the product of a strong company ethos, or how far it would differ because say, the different market conditions facing the divisions would produce different constraints and pressures or because different technologies themselves required different ways of dealing with problems and led to what might be called different managerial cultures. These were some of the questions which had to be tackled in the second stage of the study after the attitude survey had been analysed.

Substantial numbers of clerical, administrative and technical workers were among the 10,000 employed on the site, but this study is concerned only with the manual or payroll workers and their immediate supervisors, that is foremen and assistant foremen. The numbers of payroll employed on each of the five main works in 1965 is shown in Table 2.1. The Works varied considerably in size. The smallest, Works A, employed 500 and the largest, Works C, nearly 2,500.

28

Table 2.1　　Average Number of Payroll Workers
　　　　　　　Employed at Seagrass in 1965.

Works	General Workers	Tradesmen	Total
A	353	147	500
B	713	163	876
C	2,123	322	2,445
D	1,078	143	1,221
E	895	279	1,174
Other including central workshops, services, etc.	1,529	988	2,517
TOTAL SITE	6,691	2,042	8,733

To use the terminology of the company, the payroll labour force on the site divided into two groups, general workers and tradesmen. Tradesmen, about a quarter of the total, were all time-served craftsmen belonging to their appropriate trades union; that is the A.E.U., (as it then was), the E.T.U., the Boilermakers, and so on. More than a half of the tradesmen were fitters, 12 per cent were electricians, 11 per cent instrument artificers and 18 per cent plumbers, boilermakers and sheet metal workers. About 500 worked in the central workshops, while the remainder were attached to individual works for maintenance and repair activities. General workers, on the other hand, received any training they might require for work at Seagrass on the site itself after recruitment. The category of general workers included both men doing straightforward labouring jobs, as well as highly skilled chemical process workers. Most of the general workers belonged to the T.G.W.U.[1]

Our first task in planning the attitude survey was to decide what was the characteristic production technology of each of the works. After preliminary observation and discussions with management a classification was made following the Woodward system (Table 2.2). Works A and C presented very sharp contrasts in production technology.

1　The company did not operate a closed shop but manual workers were encouraged to join a trade union when first engaged.

Table 2.2.   A Classification of the Technology of the Seagrass Works[1]

Works A.	The continuous flow production of liquids and gases. Woodward category IX.
Works B.	The continuous flow production of a solid substance. Woodward category IX.
Works C.	First batch chemical production followed by the production of large batches of yarn and fibre by machine. Woodward category VIII + V.
Works D.	Production of large batches of solid substances in a number of separate plants; production of large batches of solid substances on assembly lines; production by continuous flow of solid substances and powders. Woodward categories VI + VIII + IX.
Works E.	Production of large batches of solid substances. Woodward category VIII.

[1] Following J. Woodward, 1965, op. cit. p.39.

To visit Works A was to visit a pure continuous-flow process plant as described by Blauner.

"There are no recognizable machines and very few workers visible. . . The flow of materials; the combination of different chemicals; and the temperature, pressure, and speed of the processes are regulated by automatic control devices."[1]

To visit the main part of Works C was, however, to visit any large textile spinning plant. The machines were physically alike in appearance and the sequence of activities was similar. Lines of automatic spinning and drawing machines filled the rooms, tended by operators who performed routine tasks of feeding and unloading them.

Workers on all five works were interviewed in the attitude survey and it was on Works A and C that the extremes of attitudes towards certain aspects of the employment situation were found. Curiously, however, on Works B, which according to the classification of technology appeared to be like Works A with the exception that the final product was solid, the expressed attitudes of the workers fell somewhere between the extremes of Works A and C. If a simple association between attitudes and technology was to be posited, Works B appeared to be a deviant case. Since we had to limit

1   R. Blauner, 1964, op.cit., pp.124–125.

our exploration of the possible reasons for this link between attitudes and technology we decided to concentrate upon the three works, A, B, and C. A fuller examination of the production technology as well as aspects of the control systems in use on these three works was eventually undertaken. We shall not, therefore, take space here to provide a description of Works D and E. Below, however, is a description of Works A, B and C as they first appeared to us at the time of the attitude survey.

Description of the production system in the three works A, B, and C

Works A was the smallest works. In the latter part of 1965 it employed about 360 general workers, who, with few exceptions, were working continuous shifts. There were also about 150 tradesmen engaged on maintenance and repairs. Within the physical area of the works there were, in the company's terminology, eight separate and physically distinct plants, which between them, produced twelve different products. All of them were liquid or gaseous and when the manufacturing cycle was completed were piped away. Except when sampling for quality checks, the operators never saw a raw material or an end product. About 25 per cent of the output of the works was piped away to other works on the Seagrass site and another 40 per cent was sold to works belonging to the parent company but located elsewhere. The remainder was sold on the market. Over two thirds of the general workers were engaged in tasks which required them to monitor the equipment, to read dials and charts and to adjust the valves and furnaces. These tasks were mostly performed in the control room of the plants, although some took the men outside, among the structure of pipes and columns. A group of ancillary workers such as tradesmens' mates, riggers, slingers, laboratory testers were also employed among the different plants. In practice, the plants on Works A ran continuously for a year or more.

The physical area of Works B contained five distinct production plants. As we noted the initial classification placed Works B with Works A as a continuous flow chemical works, but further study revealed certain major differences between Works A and B. It is true that on four of the plants on Works B, the process was continuous in that raw materials, piped from Works A, were fed in at the beginning of the process and there was a continuous flow of product at the end. Unlike the products of Works A, however, the Works B products were solid and granular. In addition, a number of varieties of the basic material were produced and changes of variety could result in the whole process stopping and re-starting, sometimes as often as once a week. Moreover, the nature of the chemical process itself was such that minor unscheduled stoppages might be even more frequent. These relatively frequent scheduled and unscheduled stoppages were in marked contrast to the longer runs on Works A. The fifth plant on Works B manufactured a different product with a very different process from the other four, but, in 1965, it could not have been responsible for any peculiar features of Works B because it accounted for only 5 per cent of total employment on the works.

Because of the solid nature of the products of Works B and the kind of customers to whom they were sold, there was a large finishing and warehouse section. Here the varieties were graded, bagged and packed. Most sales were to ordinary market customers although other parts of the company were still the works' largest single customer. There were about 700 general workers distributed among the plants and finishing sections of Works B and most of them were working continuous shifts. About 160 tradesmen were employed on the works. Almost one half of the general workers were concerned with the chemical process, a quarter were working in the finishing sections and another quarter in ancillary jobs, of the kind encountered on Works A. Most of the men on the chemical process itself were responsible for monitoring jobs of a kind very similar to those described above for Works A, although a few at the end of the process were operating machines which chopped the polymer. In the warehouse section the tasks consisted mainly of filling, bagging and loading.

Both Works A and B were handling highly inflammable materials, so that special methods of maintenance as well as strict safety regulations to control smoking and the wearing of protective clothing had to be enforced. Failure to comply with these regulations could result in dismissals.

Works C was unlike either Works A or B. The initial stage of manufacture was a batch chemical process which produced twenty varieties of a product which in form was not unlike that produced in Works B. But the main chemical process involved the use of eleven similar trains of equipment, each train operating on a batch basis with a cycle of approximately six hours. Consecutive runs of the same variety of product might be made for a week or more before change over. The solid product was chopped and bagged at the end of the chemical process and some was marketed at this stage. The major portion of the output continued for further processing either in the filament yarn or staple fibre section of the works. In the staple fibre section the yarn was subject to drawing and then chopped into short lengths. The resulting fibre was despatched to the customer in large bales. In the filament yarn section the spun yarn was also drawn and then wound onto bobbins on frames similar to those in use in the cotton industry. The resulting bobbins passed through a fairly large inspection section before despatch. There were 50 to 60 different types of staple fibre, and 80 different types of yarn being marketed at the time of our field work. Variations of product, particularly on

32

the filament yarn side, could, as we shall see later, have considerable impact upon the nature of the operatives' work.[1]

Works C was the largest works. At the end of 1965 it employed over 2,100 general workers, mostly on continuous shifts. The tradesmen numbered about 320. Eighteen per cent of the general workers were employed in the chemical process section. Many of the tasks here were of the same monitoring kind as on Works A, but there were also jobs of a machine minding character at the chopping and bagging stage. A fifth of the general workers worked in the staple fibre section, but the majority, 46 per cent, were working in the filament yarn section where the jobs involved machine minding and were machine paced. For example in the draw twist area of the filament yarn section, the operatives had to string up the machines, patrol them and doff the bobbins when they were full. The remaining 15 per cent of general workers on Works C were engaged in ancillary jobs. One thing which became clear as our knowledge of the Works grew, was that a superficial similarity of technology may be misleading. Initially, both Works A and B had been allocated to Woodward's category IX under the general heading of "continuous flow". Further examination revealed important differences between Works A and B which had not, at first, been apparent either to the research workers or to the company representatives with whom they discussed the matter. Most people recognised that the physical nature of the product on Works B dictated a large packaging and handling section where the tasks were completely different from those in the chemical section. What was not so well recognised was that the frequent changes of variety of product and the stopping and starting of runs in the chemical area posed problems for production planning and control of a quite different kind from those encountered on Works A. We discuss later, in Chapter 4, some of the consequences for the nature of the jobs which individual workers had to perform. In Chapter 7 we examine the way in which these differences required different control systems for dealing with product variation and how these control systems in turn imposed different constraints upon the activities of both workers and supervisors.

This general picture of the three Works provides a background for an account of the attitudes of the workers as they were revealed by the attitude survey.

---

1 See Chapter 4, p. 81

3 A Comparison of Attitudes and Behaviour

The attitude survey among the payroll workers at Seagrass was carried out in the latter part of 1965. For almost two months a small team of researchers lived in the area and although the actual interviews were carried out on the site in working time this period provided a welcome opportunity to get to know something of the community in which the workers lived. About one in twenty of the male payroll workers were interviewed personally. The response rate was high, almost 92 per cent. A cynic might say this was because the selected men were getting time off, with pay, to be interviewed and although there was some element of truth in this there was also evidence that the opportunity to talk about matters which were close to the men's experience and interests was very welcome.

The sample was designed to facilitate comparisons between the five main works. A variable sampling fraction was used to oversample general workers in the smaller works, and the results were reweighted to obtain the answers for general workers on the whole site. Table 3.1 shows the size of the initial and of the responding sample. The responding sample matched the total population extremely well in respect of those characteristics which we were

Table 3.1   The Seagrass sample of payroll workers

	Initial sample		Responding sample	
Tradesmen		156		151
General Workers:				
Works A	55		53	
Works B	55		54	
Works C	52		51	
Works D	53		40	
Works E	56		49	
Other	41		40	
Total		312		287
Total tradesmen and general workers		468		438

able to compare, that is, age, length of service, job grade, and occupation. In the following discussion attention is concentrated upon the results for the three Works selected for intensive study (Works A, B and C) and upon the attitude of general workers as a whole on the site compared with those of the tradesmen.

The interviews, which were structured, explored five broad aspects of the employment situation; first, the attitudes of the workers to the company in general as an employer; second, their attitudes towards the management on the site; third, their attitudes towards their immediate supervision; fourth, their attitudes towards the work task itself; and fifth, attitudes towards pay. Information was collected from company records about labour turnover, absenteeism and the incidence of industrial disputes on the different Works.

Attitudes towards the Company as an employer

In their attitudes towards the Company as an employer, all workers were remarkably alike. When asked to name the best things about working for the company, the four most frequently mentioned items were the security of employment, the good physical working conditions, the fringe benefits (such as, sick pay and pensions), and the welfare amenities (such as, canteens, clothing and lockers). (Table 3.2).

Table 3.2.   Unprompted answers to the question "What are some of the things you like best about working for (name of company)?"

Answers*	Tradesmen	Works A	B	C	All General Workers
		Percentages			
Job security	26	37	28	29	29
Good amenities and facilities	32	13	33	22	23
Good welfare schemes, sick pay, pensions, etc.	31	31	37	35	31
Good working conditions	30	28	37	27	21
Good money	10	11	7	12	12
An interesting job	10	20	2	6	5

*   More than one answer could be given so the answers may total to more than 100 per cent.

One small difference was that the Works A men less often spoke of the good amenities and as many as one in five said the best thing about Seagrass was the fact that they had an interesting job. Very few of the general workers on Works B or C referred to this aspect of their employment at this point. All groups however laid stress on the value of security of employment, and, further, in reply to a direct question, the great majority said they felt their job was 'very secure' or 'secure'. Only on Works B did as many as a fifth refer to feelings of insecurity. This was almost certainly a direct response to the automation and reorganization on Works B which had occurred shortly before the field work and which had led to job changes with consequent feelings of uncertainty.[1]

The tradesmen and the general workers however, offered rather different reasons for feeling so secure. The tradesmen emphasized the importance of their own skills and competence and the fact that these were in short supply.

"I'm doing my job—they need me—and that's that!" (Anglesmith)

"They're crying out for 'tiffies' (Instrument artificier)

"There'll always be a demand for my trade" (Welder)

The implication was that as craftsmen they could get a job anywhere and that they knew the company was having difficulty in recruiting the skilled labour it required. The general workers, on the other hand, tended to offer the general position of the company as their reason for feeling secure. They referred to the expansion going on around them on the site, the company's international reputation and its policy of avoiding redundancy wherever possible. This policy was known to have a long history. Another site in the area belonging to the company had kept operating at a fairly high level between the two world wars and therefore during the depression. There was undoubtedly still a fund of goodwill towards the company because it had succeeded at that time in maintaining its employment level when other industries in the area were dismissing workers right and left.

"When you read (name of company) reports you feel yourself it's a firm that you can feel secure in." (General worker, Works B)

"Well, during the depression the (name of company) kept going. The old men have told me this and if there's redundancy they'll try and get you jobs in other plants." (General worker, Works C)

---

1 See Chapter 6, p.114.

36

Most of the sample appeared to have fairly positive feelings towards their employment with the company. Nearly three quarters said that they would recommend people to come and work at Seagrass. Most thought that when men left the company it was to seek higher pay elsewhere, rather than for any other reasons, although there was a tendency for the tradesmen and the men on Works A and B to offer this explanation more frequently than the general workers on Works C. This probably reflects the fact that these groups were themselves generally less satisfied with their pay. The tradesmen were well aware that more highly-paid work with contractors was readily available nearby or even on the site itself, where a lot of construction was going on. They were also aware that such employment lacked security and did not carry any fringe benefits. But the almost daily contact they had with the contractors men, in pubs for instance, contributed to their feelings of dissatisfaction with their own pay. As for Works A and B, the earnings of the general workers were lower than those in Works C. We shall return to this point later.

Eighty-three per cent of all general workers said that they wished to stay with the company until they retired or at least 'as far as they could see'. Half of the workers in each of the three works, when asked, said that they had never thought of leaving. There was little variation in the reasons for wanting to stay. A quarter mentioned the attraction of the fringe benefits and the employment security provided by the company. But as many as a half gave purely personal reasons such as their age or a reluctance to uproot their families. The tradesmen, on the other hand, were much less tied to Seagrass. Nearly a fifth said that they definitely wanted to leave the company, and only rather more than a fifth said that they had 'never' thought of leaving the company. Of those who wished to stay with the company at *least* 'as far as they could see', 36 per cent gave negative reasons for staying—that 'nothing better had turned up yet' or 'things at work might improve in the future'.

The question "what are some of the things you like least about working for the company" produced a wide range of replies and more variation among the groups than the previous question about the things liked most. (Table 3.3). One of the 'worst things' for the tradesmen was the bonus system. Their bonus was calculated quite differently from that of the general workers and it gave rise to a number of complaints and generated strong feelings.[1] About 10 per cent of the tradesmen also found the grading system for tradesmen one of the worst features of working at Seagrass. A small but significant group of both tradesmen and general workers complained about some aspect of

---

1   See Chapter 7, p.131.

Table 3.3   Unprompted answers to the question "What are some of the things you like least about working for (name of company)?"

Answers*	Tradesmen	Works A	B	C	All General Workers
		Percentages			
Bad management	20	20	30	18	24
Regimentation, anonymity	27	20	26	16	21
Bonus system	22	4	2	2	3
Grading, category system[1]	11	2	2	–	1
Working conditions	12	2	2	10	11
Poor money, differentials	10	13	13	8	8
Shift work	2	7	6	8	6
'A bad atmosphere here'	11	6	7	2	2
Poor communications	5	6	4	4	3
Poor promotion prospects, favouritism	9	11	2	8	5
No complaints	7	11	15	12	15
Other answers[2]	21	26	30	33	27

*   More than one answer could be given so the answers may total to more than 100 per cent.

[1]   These systems are explained on p.54-55 this chapter.

[2]   A wide variety of replies, none of which was mentioned by more than three per cent.

earnings, while some tradesmen and some of the general workers in Works C complained about bad working conditions. The major objection (offered by between a fifth and a quarter) of all groups, however, centred on bad management and feelings of regimentation.

"The remoteness of communications which make you feel like a cog in a very large wheel" (Electrician)

"I did two years National Service—I find it damned hard to see the difference" (General worker, Works A)

"I feel I'm just a number. A foreman said this the other day—he agreed I was just a number and could be struck out!" (General worker, Works B)

The emphasis upon feelings of anonymity came as a surprise to the researchers but they found frequent spontaneous references to this same problem in replies to other questions. So a special analysis was made to see what percentage of the sample spoke of red tape, regimentation and anonymity at some time or another during the course of the interview. This showed that about 40 per cent of the sample were conscious and critical of impersonality on the site. (Table 3.4).

Table 3.4.   Spontaneous reference to 'red tape', regimentation, impersonality, etc., anywhere in the interview.

Answers	Tradesmen	Works A	B	C	All General Workers
		Percentages			
No reference to red tape, regimentation, impersonality	53	61	55	66	63
Spontaneous mention of red tape, regimentation, impersonality	46	38	45	34	36
Total:	100	100	100	100	100

From this discussion we can build up a picture of what the workers felt generally about the company. There was little variation among the general workers or between them and the tradesmen as to the good things about the company. Emphasis was placed upon the value of security in its broadest sense, both of employment and of the maintenance of income in adversity by the system of fringe benefits. Bad aspects of the company were said to be bad management in a general sense and the impersonality of the organization. On questions of whether they felt their job to be secure and whether they would

39

stay or leave, the tradesmen emerged as a much more independent group than the general workers. They relied more on their own ability and qualifications to keep them in a job, and so, if we can trust what they said in reply to these questions,[1] this made them more likely to leave the company. No attempt was made to get the sample to rate the company overall, as an employer—for instance by comparing it with other employers. Thus there is no simple means of summarizing whether the general attitudes to the company were 'favourable' or 'unfavourable'. But, despite some very real and vocal criticisms, there was an underlying degree of contentment and indeed positive enthusiasm about some important aspects of the company as an employer.

Attitudes towards senior management

As well as criticizing bad management spontaneously and in a general sense, all groups were alike in having a large number of men who, when asked directly, thought that management worker relations could be improved. The tradesmen, however, were more critical than the general workers (Table 3.5).

Table 3.5   "Do you think the relationship between management and workers could be improved or not?"

Answers	Tradesmen	Works A	B	C	All General Workers
			Percentages		
Yes	78	60	65	59	58
No	17	34	20	31	33
Don't know	5	6	15	10	9
Total:	100	100	100	100	100

We will discuss the general workers first. Although the porportion in all three works who thought that management worker relations could be improved was similar, the suggestions about how improvements could be effected, varied. Works A and B laid most emphasis on the need to reduce

---

1   For a discussion of the turnover of tradesmen and general workers see this Chapter, p.61–62.

what they saw as the status consciousness of the management. Over 50 per cent made comments such as,

> "Management (should) come off their high horses and meet people on the level—not think they're God" (General worker, Works B)

> "If the management stopped being so toffee nosed when they walked by" (General worker, Works A)

Although a third of the Works C respondents also complained of status-consciousness on the part of the management the main body of their criticism centred on the difficulty of access to management and the need for better communications in general.

> "Only yesterday I found out who my manager was" (this man had more than five years service) (General worker, Works C)

> "You can't approach management direct—there's too many inter-mediate people" (General worker, Works C)

Whereas over 50 per cent of the Works C men complained of basic communication difficulties, such problems were mentioned by only a quarter of the men in works A and B.

Some of these differences between the works fell into place when the actual pattern of contact at work between the men and the individuals they thought of as senior management was established. Far more of the men in Works A had actually been in contact with management and particularly with levels of management above that of plant manager (Table 3.6). In Works C, for instance, 39 per cent of the general workers said they never came into contact with senior management compared with only 11 per cent in Works A. Over a quarter in Works A had had some contact with the works engineer compared with only 8 per cent in Works C. Not unexpectedly then, the majority of men in Works A thought that they saw enough of management in the course of their work whereas between 30 and 40 per cent in Works B and C complained that they did not. At the time when this study was made, it seems clear that for some reason—whether it was that the technology required closer involvement of senior and middle management in the running of the plant, whether because some works were smaller than others, or whether as a result of deliberate management policy—the general workers in Works A did see a lot more of their management than the general workers in Works B and

41

Table 3.6. "Do you ever come in contact with senior management in the course of your work?"

Answers	Tradesmen	Works A	B	C	All General Workers
		Percentages			
Yes	77	89	65	59	65
No	23	11	35	39	34
Don't know	–	–	–	2	1
Total	100	100	100	100	100
The person with whom there is contact*					
(in order of seniority)					
No one	23	11	35	39	35
Shift Manager	1	6	–	–	1
Plant Manager	12	56	44	31	31
Works Engineer	56	28	15	8	14
Others	16	22	20	24	24
Don't know	–	–	–	2	2

* More than one answer could be given so the answers may add up to more than 100 per cent.

C. But those who saw a lot of senior management were as likely to be critical of their relationships as those who saw a little. The differences lay, as we saw above, in the suggestions made to improve the position.

Real differences emerged between the three works in reply to another question which was: "Here are two opposing views about industry generally. I'd like you to tell me which you agree with more. Some people say that a firm is like a football side—because good teamwork means success and is to everyone's advantage. Others say that teamwork in industry is impossible—because employers and men are really on opposite sides. Which view do you agree with more?" Only 57 per cent of the general workers in Works C answered in 'teamwork' terms compared with 78 and 81 per cent of Works B and A respectively.[1] (Table 3.7). Willener, who first published replies to this question in a survey carried out among French workers, suggested that it reveals whether men see employer-worker relations in fundamentally 'oppositional' or 'co-operational' terms.[2]

Table 3.7. "Here are two opposing views about industry generally. I'd like you to tell me which you agree with more. Some people say that a firm is like a football side—because teamwork means success and is to everyone's advantage. Others say that teamwork in industry is impossible—because employers and men are really on opposite sides. Which view do you agree with more?"

| Answers | Tradesmen | Works | | | All General Workers |
| | | A | B | C | |
		Percentages			
Football team	71	81	78	57	69
Opposite sides	22	15	17	33	23
Not answered/ don't know	6	4	6	10	8
Total:	100	100	100	100	100

His argument implied that there was a link between the worker's general image of society and his view of workplace relationships. Our respondents had not been asked directly why they chose the 'teamwork' alternative or

[1] The percentage of 'co-operational' replies from the continuous-process works is close to the percentage of similar replies given by Goldthorpe's assembly-line workers. Goldthorpe et al., 1968, p.73.
[2] A. Willener "Payment Systems in the French Steel and Iron Mining Industry: An exploration in Managerial Resistance to Change" p.609 in ed. G. K. Zollschan and Walter Hirsch *Explorations in Social Change*, H. M. Co., Boston, 1964. See also, J. Goldthorpe, 1966, op.cit., p.238. It is interesting to note that the football team analogy also makes its apeal to management "The role of a company chairman was like that of a football team manager but unlike the captain of a football team" said Mr. Joe Hyman, then Chairman of Viyella International. *Financial Times,* 14th February, 1968.

vice versa, but if spontaneous comments were made these were recorded verbatim. About a half of the men in all three works did so. Many were so general as to defy analysis—e.g.

"Teamwork comes into it a lot"

"You must have teamwork", etc.,

These remarks might be taken to imply a general acceptance of the cooperational view about how "it ought to be". However, amidst the generalities there were a few examples where men in Works A and B made specific reference to the demands of the task as the reason for their choice:—

"In our (work) place if its working well that's because we are working as a team and that's how it ought to be." (General worker, Works B)

"You must have teamwork—especially over a job like this. On big upsets (the) management muck in with you at once." (General worker, Works A)

No comments at all of this kind were recorded by the general workers on Works C. They were much more likely to interpret the question in 'oppositional' terms.

"Teamwork's a load of rubbish." (General worker, Works C)

"The firm's out for its own ends—they'd give the workers a handful of rice if they could get away with it!" (General worker, Works C)

Such replies are more characteristic of what has been called the 'traditional' working class image of the work situation, where workers are directly conscious of conflict arising from a fundamental dichotomy of interests between employer and employed.

Our data suggest, in fact, that at least two levels of perception existed. We have seen that the Works A men shared with the Works C general workers a critical view of management worker relations in general and they were certainly aware of conflicts of interest over things like pay. They too might at one level, have seen work relations in oppositional or conflict terms. But in reply to a question which asked about 'teams', they were primarily influenced by what they directly experienced as the demands of the particular production system which they were operating. If the technology on Works A was

44

such that it required more frequent contact between management and men to keep the plants running the operators could quite naturally see themselves as part of a team. The Works C men, on the other hand, were not only aware of the possibility of conflict about issues like pay, but also felt the production situation itself to be fraught with conflict. [1] In neither case would we feel confident that the question was exploring a general view of class relationships, but rather the responses of workers to the immediate work situation.

So far the discussion has centred upon the attitudes of the general workers towards management. The views of the tradesmen were rather different. In the course of their work they saw management almost as frequently as Works A general workers and yet they were more critical than Works A of management-worker relations in general, and slightly more likely to say that they did not see enough of management in the course of their work. (Tables 3.5 and 3.6). They attached less importance than the general workers in Works A and B to a reduction of status-consciousness and more social mixing on the part of management as a way of meeting their criticisms. Instead, well over a half saw more visits to the shop floor and easier access to management as a way of improving relations. The tradesmen have already been shown to be more independent and less likely to be committed to the company as an employer. [2] This attitude might contribute to the fact that few of them desired closer personal relations with management. They preferred instead to emphasize the need for more contact in the context of carrying out the job.

Of all the groups the tradesmen were strongest in their criticism of management worker relations, which might lead one to expect that this group of traditional craft workers would view the firm in 'oppositional' terms. But only a few made observations like:

"The capitalists are on one side of the fence and we're on the other."

In fact over 70 per cent of the tradesmen supported the team work view. (Table 3.7).

---

1. One of our colleagues, Celia Davies, of Imperial College, explored these possible different levels of interpretation when putting this same question to a sample of manual workers in a batch engineering company. She confirms that a significant group of her respondents felt that there *should* be teamwork but that there was not because of poor planning or communication by management. Yet another group consciously recognised that they were not consistently in one team with management on all issues. Production might involve teamwork, but there was conflict over pay.
2. See this Chapter, p.37.

There was little to suggest that this was based upon what they perceived to be the demands of the immediate work situation which was the important factor for the general workers. Rather the tradesmen were explicitly expressing a more general 'unitary' view of the employment relationship emphasizing the identity of shared interests. [1]

> "The question answers itself—it's to everyone's advantage."

> "More profits—better for workers because of the profit-sharing scheme."

Even when they were less positive they said things like:

> "I'd like the top one (teamwork) but it doesn't always come out like that. Sometimes it's management's fault and sometimes the men."

This was a surprising finding because the tradesmen had expressed considerable hostility to management and support for an egalitarian philosophy in the work situation. [2] But such views did not so much reflect a belief in the inevitability of conflict, as a sense of the tradesmen's own 'being' and independent worth; a belief that they were as essential to the production process as any manager and that they were equally of value as part of the team. It followed logically, then, that if everyone was working for the same goal they should all receive equal status.[3]

The replies to the teamwork question were interesting in so far as they revealed a number of different frames of reference which different groups of workers were using. Whilst the majority of both general workers and tradesmen chose to view the firm as a football team, the majority were also quite firm in their view that management worker relations could be improved.

Attitudes towards supervision

When we turned to examine attitudes to supervision we found considerable differences between the general workers. In most cases the first-line supervisor was an assistant foreman, although in a few cases it was the foreman himself. Four main questions were asked:

---

1 Alan Fox, *Industrial Sociology and Industrial Relations*, Royal Commission on Trade Unions and Employers' Associations, H.M.S.O., London, 1966, pp.2–5.
2 See Chapter 5, p.105.
3 See Chapter 5, p.105.

"Would you say you get on with your immediate superior very well, reasonably well, or not too well?"

"Does your immediate superior have enough authority to answer your questions and deal with your problems?"

"Do they choose the right men to be supervisors here?"

"Would you say that the supervision you get is adequate?"

Table 3.8.   "Would you say you get on with your immediate superior very well, reasonably well, or not too well?"

Answers	Tradesmen	Works A	Works B	Works C	All General Workers
		Percentages			
Very well	53	68	61	57	55
Reasonably well	43	23	33	33	36
Not too well	3	4	4	–	2
Poorly	–	2	–	6	3
Don't know/ Not answered	1	4	2	4	3
Total:	100	100	100	100	100

The great majority of the general workers said that they got on either very well or reasonably well with their supervisor in immediate personal terms (Table 3.8), but there was considerable variety of views on the three other questions. In every case Works C men were the most critical and Works A the most satisfied, with Works B falling in between. Forty-six per cent of Works C said their supervisor lacked authority compared with only 17 per cent of Works A (Table 3.9). The spontaneous comments made by the men in answering this question were very revealing. Given the form of the question,

Table 3.9. "Does your immediate superior have enough authority to answer your questions and deal with your problems?"

Answers	Tradesmen	Works A	B	C	All General Workers
		Percentages			
Yes	64	81	65	48	62
No	31	17	26	46	31
It varies	4	2	7	2	5
Don't know	2	–	2	4	2
Total:	100	100	100	100	100

most of the men interpreted 'authority' in terms of *job* competence. Many of the men on Works A justified their positive replies in a very simple manner:

"He knows his job."

"He has *all* the authority. He runs the plant, nobody else."

The Works C respondents, on the other hand, questioned the authority of their supervisors in the same terms:

"He should (be able to answer your questions) but half of them can't—they usually say 'see the foreman'."

"He hasn't got a clue about the job," etc.

Perhaps the negative attitude on Works C was summed up by the man who said:

"Well you don't ask him any questions really. He's the same as you but he's been there longer."

Not perhaps surprisingly Works C were very critical of the method of selecting supervisors. Nearly a half of them said the right men were not chosen, compared with 31 per cent of Works B and only 19 per cent of

48

Table 3.10.   "Do they choose the right men to be supervisors here?"

Answers	Tradesmen	Works A	B	C	All General Workers
		Percentages			
Yes	19	44	30	24	31
Sometimes only	30	29	30	26	24
No	48	19	31	48	38
Don't know	4	8	9	2	6
Total:	100	100	100	100	100

Works A. (Table 3.10). As for quality, only 20 per cent of Works C described their supervision as very adequate compared with 40 per cent of Works A. (Table 3.11).

The tradesmen also said that they got on well with their supervisors, but their views about the quality and authority of supervision were rather like

Table 3.11.   "Would you say that the supervision you get is very adequate, adequate or not adequate?"

Answers	Tradesmen	Works A	B	C	All General Workers
		Percentages			
Very adequate	24	40	24	20	22
Adequate	53	42	52	60	55
Not very adequate	} 20	4	9	4	5
Inadequate		12	6	16	12
Varies	–	2	4	–	2
Don't know	3	–	6	–	3
Total:	100	100	100	100	100

those of Works B, that is not so enthusiastic as Works A but less critical than Works C. Like Works C, however, they were also very critical of the method of selection of supervisors. Nearly a half said the right men were not selected. Yet as is illustrated by Table 3.12, the tradesmen and Works C operatives had some differences of emphasis in the qualities they sought in a supervisor. All groups thought that it was important for a supervisor to know his job. But

Table 3.12. Unprompted answers to the question "What qualities do you think are most important for (title of immediate superior)?"

Answers*	Tradesmen	Works			All General Workers
		A	B	C	
		Percentages			
To know his job	71	55	54	43	48
To be able to get on with the men	31	38	19	20	29
Qualities of organization and leadership	54	68	70	37	46
Other personal qualities[1]	29	34	33	37	34
Other answers	2	4	6	12	5

* More than one answer could be given so the answers may total to more than 100 per cent.

[1] These included patience, tolerance, a sense of humour, etc., etc.

whereas about a half of the general workers put this forward, no less than 70 per cent of the tradesmen named this quality. Because of their pride in their own competence, the tradesmen insisted that anyone who was to supervise them must be judged to be competent as well. Ability to organize and to provide leadership while still important for tradesmen was relatively more important for the general workers in Works A and B.

Similar stringent safety rules were applied on both Works A and B, but the men on Works B were rather more likely to say that there were 'too many' rules for employees. Moreover, in reply to a question about whether discipline was too strict, Works B was much the most critical, no less than

35 per cent of the sample complaining that it was too strict, compared with 16 per cent in Works C and only 6 per cent in Works A. The tradesmen were more likely than the general workers in any of the three works to say there were 'too many' rules. But on the subject of discipline they were closer to Works A and C and not so critical as Works B.

Attitudes to the work task

When asked about their actual job, the views of the men on Works A and Works C were very much in contrast (Table 3.13). On this question the attitudes of Works B fell closer to those of Works C. Over 70 per cent of the Works A men found their jobs interesting. We noted above that many of them

Table 3.13.　"Generally speaking, do you find your job is interesting, about average, or boring?"

Answers	Tradesmen	Works A	B	C	All General Workers
		Percentages			
Interesting	39	72	39	26	45
About average	32	15	22	31	25
Boring	13	6	26	27	21
It varies	16	8	13	16	11
Total:	100	100	100	100	100

spoke of this as one of the best things about working for the company. Overwhelmingly they said that there was nowhere else, either on the particular plant they were in, nor anywhere else on the Seagrass site, that they would rather work. Not only did a quarter of the men in Works B and C describe their jobs as boring, but 29 per cent in Works C and 43 per cent in Works B would have preferred to work elsewhere in their own plants, although the reason most often given was the better money obtainable in other jobs. This reaction was natural because there was a greater diversity of jobs on these two works which was associated with a wider range of earnings. Indeed, at the time of the field work, there was a natural system of promotion in Works B whereby men were recruited first into the warehouse and bagging section and then progressed into the chemical process areas, where pay was higher because the jobs were more highly graded.

Table 3.14. "Does the job give you a chance to try out ideas of your own?"

Answers	Tradesmen	Works A	B	C	All General Workers
		Percentages			
Yes or sometimes	53	45	22	32	31
Rarely	17	23	24	20	18
Never	30	32	54	49	51
Total:	100	100	100	100	100

Finding jobs interesting seemed to be related to the ability to exercise discretion on the job. Nearly half of Works B and C respondents said they could never try out their own ideas compared with only a third of Works A (Table 3.14). Over a fifth in both Works B and C said that they didn't have enough freedom on the job compared with only 9 per cent of Works A (Table 3.15).

Table 3.15. "Do you have enough freedom on the job? Do you think too much is left to you, you don't have enough say, or is it about right?"

Answers	Tradesmen	Works A	B	C	All General Workers
		Percentages			
Too much is left to me	3	2	6	2	4
I don't have enough say	32	9	22	22	23
It's about right	60	79	69	67	67
Varies	5	9	4	10	6
Total:	100	100	100	100	100

There were also some interesting contrasts between the tradesmen and the general workers as a whole in attitudes to the work task. On average, the tradesmen were less likely than the general workers to describe their jobs as positively boring but also less likely than the Works A men to describe them as positively interesting. It was rather that they took it for granted that their kind of skilled work should be interesting (Table 3.13). 'Craft competence' was frequently mentioned as a reason:

"It's a good class of work" (Turner)

"I always *make* it interesting, I like to do a good job" (Electrician)

The tradesmen more frequently said that their jobs gave them a chance to try out ideas of their own (Table 3.14), but a third of the tradesmen said that they didn't have enough say on the job (Table 3.15), implying that they knew how to do the job but found their efforts frustrated in some way. This frustration was quite clearly expressed in comments made on these questions, even by men who said they could try out their own ideas.

"Well you can try them (ideas) out but you musn't broadcast it" (Electrician)

"Unofficially—when they (ideas) work and they are alright I tell them and it's O.K. but I'm not supposed to do this." (Artificer)

Similar complaints were made by the tradesmen who felt they didn't have enough freedom on the job.

"No, I think that's one big reason why so many men are leaving. There's little opportunity to use initiative. On average I think there must be two gaffers for every five men." (Fitter)

"I have to go and tell the foreman all the time and then wait two days for his decision." (Electrician)

Other differences of attitude between the tradesmen and general workers arose in answers to two more questions, 'Are you told enough in advance about things to do with your work?', and 'Are you told enough about things happening in the plant generally?'. Nearly two thirds of the tradesmen felt that they were inadequately informed compared to less than a half of the general workers. This again suggests that the craftsmen felt the need to be treated more as equals and to be respected because of their craft competence.

53

Attitudes to pay

A matter of prime importance for any worker and one which may well colour his other views of the job is the level of pay. Basic rates of pay at Seagrass were determined centrally by negotiation at company level with the unions concerned. For the general workers, the company system of job appraisement was in operation over the whole of the Seagrass site. All jobs on the site were evaluated on the basis of the skill, physical and intellectual effort, and the possible adverse conditions involved in doing the job and allocated to a category from 0–14. These categories automatically carried an hourly differential above the basic rate. The distribution of job categories in a works was dictated by the process itself, and some works carried a higher proportion of high category jobs. At the same time a multi-factor bonus system was in operation. There was a bonus maximum of approximately 27 per cent of basic pay in operation over the whole site. But certain groups of workers were occasionally able to exceed this maximum while on the other hand there might well be variations in the opportunity to earn bonus, so that bonus could also fail to reach the maximum. Opportunities to work overtime and extra shifts also varied from time to time between works.

Table 3.16.   Previous week's gross earnings[1]

Answers	Tradesmen	Works A	B	C	All General Workers
		Percentages			
Up to £15	7	4	9	6	9
£15 up to £17	3	4	7	6	9
£17 up to £20	21	59	52	27	37
£20 up to £25	30	15	28	39	30
£25 and over	35	15	4	22	14
D.K.	4	4	–	–	1
Total:	100	100	100	100	100

[1] When the replies of the sample to the question "What were your earnings last week?" and "What do you earn on average?" were compared with information about actual earnings provided by the company (by permission of the respondents), "previous week's earnings" were found to be a more reliable guide to actual earnings.

Unlike the general workers, a tradesmen's *initial* grading depended on his own personal skill rather than the job he was doing. All tradesmen were given a grade from A to D, on which the basic rate of pay depended. Bonus rates, however, were set by an estimator on the basis of the particular job to be done. The bonus was a source of bitter complaint from the tradesmen, and as we have seen, over a fifth mentioned it as the 'worst thing' about the company. Many tradesmen thought that bonus changes were the most important improvement that could be made at Seagrass.

There were considerable variations in the earnings of the general workers in the three works (Table 3.16). The Works C men were earning the most. More than a fifth were earning upwards of £25 a week compared with 15 per cent on Works A and only 4 per cent on Works B. Twice as many were earning more than £20 a week on Works C as on Works A. There was general criticism of pay levels among the whole sample but, not surprisingly, we found that the men on Works C were far less critical of their pay than on the other two works (Table 3.17). Only 29 per cent described their pay as unreasonable compared with 42 per cent on Works A and 59 per cent on Works B. They were also rather more likely than the other two works to say that there were no other firms in the neighbourhood which would pay more than the company at Seagrass.

The level of the tradesmen's earnings was considerably higher than that of the general workers as a whole, and even higher than the Works C earnings. They were, however, as critical of their rate of pay as the general workers. We have already seen that the tradesmen tended to compare their pay with that of craftsmen working for the contractors and it was the contractors who were most frequently cited by the many tradesmen who thought that other firms in the neighbourhood would pay them more than the rate they were getting at Seagrass (Table 3.17). The Tradesmen's criticisms were compounded from two sources. One was the irritation of knowing that more money was available elsewhere, even if it did lack the other advantages of Seagrass employment, and second their strong sense of their own worth.

General workers and tradesmen alike viewed favourably, however, two other important aspects of their market situation at Seagrass. These were the pension scheme and the provision whereby the company would make up National Insurance sickness benefit to the level of basic pay when the men were off sick. These provisions were generous compared with those generally available for manual workers at this time. The sick pay scheme provided four weeks benefit after six months service, scaling up to twenty-six weeks of sickness and twenty-six weeks of industrial injury benefit for those with more than three years service. Over 80 per cent of both categories thought the sick

Table 3.17. "For the sort of work you do here would you say your take-home pay is:?"

Answers	Tradesmen	Works A	Works B	Works C	All General Workers
		Percentages			
Very reasonable	6	9	2	16	8
Reasonable	53	47	39	56	49
Unreasonable	40	42	59	29	41
Don't know	1	2	–	–	2
Total:	100	100	100	100	100

"Do you know of any firms around here which would pay you more?"

Answers*	Tradesmen	Works A	Works B	Works C	All General Workers
		Percentages			
Yes					
Contractors	46	28	35	23	27
Steel Works	12	11	6	10	11
Other	13	15	6	10	9
No	32	42	43	55	47
Don't know	3	8	11	4	8

* More than one answer could be given so the answers may total to more than 100 per cent.

pay arrangements and the pension provisions were reasonable or very reasonable. There was also general support for the company profit sharing scheme, 69 per cent of the tradesmen and 82 per cent of the general workers offering unqualified approval. A certain suspicion showed through when reasons were advanced for the company having introduced the scheme:

"Sharing out to avoid tax I would say"

"To make you vote Conservative—and it worked."

"To avoid the Company being nationalized."

Others, however, doubtful of whether the objects had been achieved, thought the scheme had been introduced:

"To keep workers here and happy."

"To make them feel part of the company."

"To make them feel they are working for themselves."

Summary of Attitudes

The significant finding in this exploration of attitudes was in the position of the tradesmen. They did not differ markedly from the general workers in their attitudes towards the company as an employer—they shared the general approval of the good working conditions, the security and the fringe benefits. They were also critical of management worker relations in general. But their reasons for adopting these attitudes differed from those of the general workers. In various ways the tradesmen were expressing a sense of their own worth and independence which stemmed from their consciousness of their own skill. This was also reflected in their criticism of the choice of supervisors, the discipline imposed upon them and what they felt to be the lack of autonomy given to them on the job. It is consistent with this picture of the tradesmen that generally they had more decided views than the general workers. They less often offered 'don't know' in reply to a question. For instance when asked "We have talked now about quite a number of things which you like and dislike about work here. What do you think are the most important changes that could be carried out here at Seagrass?" only 9 per cent of the tradesmen, compared with as many as a quarter of the general workers, had no suggestions to make.[1]

The main contrast in attitudes between the three groups of general workers was to be found between the pure continuous-flow process works (Works A) on the one hand and the batch production works (Works C) on the other. The differences centred not on general attitudes towards the

1 See Chapter 5, p.99.

company or 'management' in the abstract, but upon the supervisory system, the work task, and a marked difference in the extent to which the two groups took a 'co-operational' or a 'conflict' view of the firm. There were already a number of indications that these differences were in some way linked to the different tasks in which the men were engaged. But what of Works B? Basically sharing the position of the other two works in its attitudes to the company and to management, it occupied a very varied place in relation to other attitudes. The men as often took a 'co-operational' view of the firm as Works A but they were closer to Works C in their criticism of the lack of interest of the job. The question immediately arises whether the differences in the nature of the process and product which distinguished the production technology of Works B from Works A could in some way help to account for these differences of attitude. These were the kind of questions which led us to decide that a fuller exploration of the possible link between technology and attitudes were required. But first we examined some evidence about behaviour in the work situation.

Attitudes and Behaviour

The literature on the relationship between employee attitudes and behaviour is extensive. One review of that literature some fifteen years ago stated:

> "Only infrequently, however, are discussions of the correlates of employee attitudes found and these are almost never substantiated by empirical evidence." [1]

The conclusion drawn is that:

> "there is little evidence in the available literature that employee attitudes of the type usually measured in morale surveys bear any simple—or for that matter appreciable—relationship to performance on the job."

The review did however point out that job satisfaction seemed to be related in some degree to absenteeism and turnover. In other words, that in any discussion of satisfaction or morale it is important to distinguish between the forces which "affect performance on the job and those which involve with-drawal from the job (absences, accidents, turnover)". Subsequent research has

---

1 Arthur H. Brayfield and Walter H. Crockett, "Employee Attitudes and Employee Performance", *Psychological Bulletin,* Vol. 52, No.5., 1955, p.396.

not changed this picture but rather lends support to the view that there is a far more complex inter-relationship of variables than is implied in the equation of the happy or satisfied worker with the reliable, high output worker.

Certainly where attitudes towards different aspects of the employment relationship differed as markedly as at Seagrass it was by no means clear what the net effect would be. Goldthorpe's interpretation of the data for his car assembly workers, for instance, implied the striking of a compensatory balance following the specific ordering of wants which his sample displayed. What were perceived as relatively high earnings made up for a boring job and this balance was accompanied both by relatively favourable attitudes to the company, a 'co-operational' view of the employment situation and little evidence of negative behaviour in terms of high labour turnover or grievance activity, at least at the time Goldthorpe was doing his field work.[1]

In the Seagrass situation would a fairly high level of criticism of senior management by all groups of workers lead one to expect a uniform pattern of behaviour of an 'unco-operative' kind? Would the high level of criticism of immediate supervision and boredom with the job in Works C lead us to expect more unco-operative behaviour there than on Works A? And would the high degree of job satisfaction on Works A lead us to expect very positive behaviour?

One comment on terminology is required. We prefer to follow Kynaston Reeves and to speak of 'constraint evasive' behaviour rather than 'uncooperative behaviour'.[2] 'Uncooperative' carries certain value overtones. Kynaston Reeves defines constraints as: "those elements or features of an organisation which impinge on a member to determine the behaviour content of his work". The term constraint does not imply anything about the necessity for the existence of those particular elements or features of the work situation for achieving the goals of the organisation, or about the desirability of compliance with, or evasion of, the constraints, or indeed about the desirability of the goals. One interesting question might be how far particular constraints can be shown to be necessary to the objectives of the organisation as well as how far they will be perceived, by the individuals subject to them, as necessary. Will constraints imposed, say, by the specific production technology be more often perceived as necessary and therefore perhaps willingly accepted, than those imposed by the control system devised by management? From the point of view of behaviour these constraints are a

---

1 J. Goldthorpe, 1966, op. cit., p.237.
2 T. Kynaston Reeves, 1967, op. cit.

fact of life for the employee if he remains with the organisation, to be accepted positively, neutrally or evaded. The most extreme example of constraint evasive behaviour is then to leave the organisation altogether. Temporary absences from work will be a temporary evasion. Formal grievance activity involving strikes, 'go-slows' or overtime bans yet another. Informal arrangements among workers to modify formal work requirements are yet another. These various forms of constraint evasive behaviour are not necessarily inter-related, or substitutes for one another, although they may be. Certainly there is a qualitative difference between individual and collective action i.e. between the individual employee seeking alternative employment on the one hand, and joining with other workers in an attempt to change the employment conditions which he does not like, on the other.

Unless the research worker engages in some form of detailed shop or office study, it is extremely difficult to obtain a complete coverage of all these

Table 3.18.   Labour turnover and absenteeism on the Seagrass site 1964–66

	Tradesmen	Work A	B	C	All General Workers
			Percentages		
Annual Labour Turnover					
1964	10.6	9.3	8.1	7.9	10.0
1965	17.1	18.9	19.5	17.0	20.0
1966	20.9	17.8	19.4	19.2	20.9
Annual percentage lost time all causes[1]					
1964	8.1	6.0	6.0	7.6	NA
1965	8.1	5.6	6.0	7.5	NA
1966	7.6	5.2	5.8	6.8	NA

1 Absenteeism rates are not avi>able for tradesmen and general workers separately. The tradesmen figures relate to the engineering works where a quarter of all tradesmen were employed. The works' figures relate to general workers and tradesmen employed on those works.

various types of behaviour. There was no time to do this in the Seagrass study. But evidence was readily available about turnover and absenteeism rates as well as some data on the frequency of industrial disputes. (Table 3.18). These were analysed for one year on either side of the year in which the field work for the attitude survey was carried out, that is over the period 1964 to 1966.

Over these three years there was a large increase in labour turnover on the site as a whole, a doubling from 10 per cent to 20 per cent per annum. This was almost certainly influenced by the employment situation in the area which had been improving quite markedly at this time. In December 1963, the male unemployment rate was 4.3 per cent compared with a national average of 2.0 per cent. By the end of 1965 it had fallen to 2.3 per cent, that is only 0.5 per cent above the national average. In 1964, the lowest labour turnover among the general workers was on Works C, but it more than doubled in the three year period. On the other hand, labour turnover on Works A increased less than average, so that by 1966 the position of Works A and Works C had been reversed. Works A had an annual rate of 17.8 per cent compared with 19.2 per cent on Works C. Labour turnover among the tradesmen was similar to and increased pari passu over the three years with that of the general workers. It was very slightly higher than on any of the three individual works.

As labour turnover rose, however, absenteeism declined somewhat in all three works, but it was highest in Works C in 1964 and despite the decline remained highest there.[1] The company's records distinguished between certified and uncertified sickness absenteeism, accidents and "absence for all other reasons". It was in the latter category that Works C was originally highest and where it showed the biggest increase. Tradesmen had a higher absenteeism rate than the general workers in 1964 and although their rate, too, declined it was still somewhat higher in 1966.

The incidence of industrial disputes in the period 1964–1966 was varied. A T.G.W.U. overtime ban was imposed on the site in early December 1965 affecting the general workers in all five works. It had been lifted on Works A by the beginning of January but it continued in Works C until March and in Works B until April 1966. As for disputes involving loss of hours, Works A had none in the whole three year period and Works B none involving general workers and only one which involved some of the tradesmen. Works C, on the other hand, had nine walk-outs involving general workers. The issue in dispute was nearly always something to do with bonus payments. In addition to the

---

1 See footnote to Table 3.18 for a description of the precise coverage of the absenteeism figures.

dispute on Works B the tradesmen on the Seagrass site had also been involved in six other disputes in this period. They centred on such issues as working conditions, relationships with the contractors' men who were accused of taking over the tradesmen's work, as well as inter-craft disputes about demarcation.

Thus the differences in these aspects of behaviour between the three works seemed to parallel the differences in expressed attitude to the immediate work situation which the attitude survey revealed. We do not of course know whether the *individuals* who were critical on a works were those who participated in unofficial strikes or who had the highest absentee records. But Works C with the most critical attitude towards the job itself and immediate supervision, showed the largest increase in labour turnover, had the highest absenteeism rate and the worst record of industrial disputes. There was little to suggest that the high rates of pay and the men's satisfaction with those rates compensated for the unsatisfactory nature of other aspects of the job. Indeed, it might be argued that the need to preserve one good aspect of the employment situation, namely the pay, was felt all the more strongly because of other deprivations, and led to militant behaviour on this score. Works B was less critical generally, had a lower absenteeism rate and a better industrial record. Works A, which had a favourable orientation towards both the job itself and immediate supervision, consistently had the lowest level of absenteeism on the site and, apart from the overtime ban, no industrial disputes at all.

The tradesmen had an average labour turnover, a relatively high rate of absenteeism and were involved in a number of industrial disputes. Their absenteeism may have been related to their relatively high pay and their sense of independence. But unlike Works C, the tradesmen's unofficial strike activity, superficially at any rate, was directed more to preserving the viability of their own craft than directly to improving or protecting their financial situation This is consistent with the nature of the general criticisms voiced to us by the craftsmen, for these were directed towards areas where they felt their craft status and autonomy were not receiving due recognition.

Thus two quite different patterns of attitudes emerge, both of which are associated with 'constraint evasive behaviour.' The tradesmen did not find their work boring; in fact they took it for granted that it should be interesting. The tradesmen were conscious of possessing a skill which was part of their individual identity. Resentment which boiled over into overt militant behaviour, was aroused at what were viewed as encroachments upon, or insufficient recognition of, this craft status. Thus there also existed a sense of *shared* craft identity. In discussing management proposals for work reorganization which would have given certain tasks previously done by the

62

craftsmen, to the general workers, one of the leading engineering shop stewards said dramatically:

"They want us to sell our birthright for a mess of potage."

And in saying this he had the support of the representatives of the other craft unions who were present.

No such coherent feelings were discernible among the general workers. There was a separation between them as individuals and their jobs. This does not mean, however, that the general workers were not alike in some of their attitudes. We have seen that because the company satisfied their need for security they generally viewed it favourably as an employer whilst vigorously criticizing management worker relations in general. But there were marked differences between general workers in different works in their constraint evasive behaviour. And these differences seemed to be associated with certain aspects of the tasks they were doing; with the degree to which they found their jobs interesting and in the way in which they viewed their immediate relationships with their supervisors.

Thus in explaining the attitudes and behaviour of the tradesmen it appeared to be at least as important to look outside the immediate work situation as at factors within it. Meaning could be given to their response to work at Seagrass only by reference to their craft training, to their craft ethos and their sense of independence of any single employer. For the general worker, however, the evidence pointed to factors in the immediate work situation having a considerable impact upon certain attitudes and behaviour. So far attention had been concentrated upon differences between general workers in different Works. But what would an analysis by the type of work performed reveal?

4 Work Tasks and Attitudes

In the light of all the earlier studies it was appealing to think that the difference in the attitudes of Works A and Works C general workers towards the interest of their job and towards their supervisors was in some way the outcome of the different technologies of the two works. But when the results of the attitude survey were first discussed with management and unions at Seagrass an apparently much simpler explanation was offered:

"There is better management on Works A."

But could it be so simple? What, after all, was "better" management? Joan Woodward's argument was precisely that the technological constraints in the production area of continuous flow process industries were such that the management task was easier.[1] In any case, why should the quality of management affect, for instance, the interest men found in their jobs? Was this not much more likely to be linked with the actual tasks or work which they had to do in the plant?

It is obvious that however homogeneous the production system in a works, there will be a range of different jobs which individual operators occupy. We felt that we might get closer to isolating the influence of technology upon attitudes, at least in so far as that influence operated by way of specific work tasks, if we could reclassify the sample, so that irrespective of Works, men doing similar tasks were grouped together. We could then examine the pattern of attitudes which emerged.

The man-machine system

A worker experiences the production system first and foremost in terms of where he is required to be and what he is required to do during his working hours. Even the period of time he spends in the factory depends to a very large extent upon the nature of the production system. At Seagrass for example, most of the general workers were required to work shifts. The physical conditions in which work has to be carried out are largely determined by the nature of the process. Thus, at Seagrass, there were varying degrees of heat, noise and smell in the different Works. The production

---

1 See Chapter 1, p.17.

system also determines whether a worker stands in front of a machine all day pulling a handle, or whether, for example, he moves about the plant collecting samples, taking readings of temperatures, pressures etc. Moreover differing tasks will provide varying opportunities for social contact. Some will actually require cooperation between numbers of workers. Some will merely provide opportunities for social contact; yet others will be essentially solitary operations.

In looking for a basis for classifying jobs across the Works we decided initially to concentrate upon the characteristics of the task itself and what the worker was required to do on his shift.

The company used a system of job appraisement for determining job categories.[1] But these categories did not appear to lend themselves to the kind of classification we were looking for. They were intended to establish the relative worth of jobs in a system of pay differentials. Four elements— mental and physical requirements, acquired skills and working conditions— were measured and combined by a weighting system. The result was that the job of a draw twist operator in Works C was in the same category as that of a panel operator in Works A. Yet in terms of the demands made upon them by their job in the sense we were interested in, there were considerable and important differences.

In searching for an alternative classification we were influenced by a number of studies, which from different points of view have tried to reduce jobs to their 'essential' elements. One such stream has developed from the growing concern with the impact of automation upon job requirements. Crossman has defined automation as the "replacement of human information processes by mechanical ones".[2] The 'elements' in a job are then seen as the various kinds of inputs which the worker provides. Information will be one, physical effort or horsepower another. Brown has suggested that there are three fundamental abilities used in various combinations in any job.

"(1) the exertion of force or expenditure of power, (2) stereotyped motion, (3) reaction to variability."[3]

---

1 See Chapter 3, p.54.
2 E. R. F. Crossman "European Experience with the Changing Nature of Jobs due to Automation" in *The Requirements of Automated Jobs*, OECD, Paris 1965, p.161., et.seq.
3 A. Brown "Artefacts, Automation and Human Ability" in ed. J. R. Lawrence *Operational Research and the Social Sciences* Tavistock Publication, London, 1966, p.237., et.seq.

Thus a press operator is primarily a source of stereotyped motions and of energy and to a much lesser extent responds to variability. On the other hand while a surgeon primarily responds to variability, that is to environmental information, through the exercise of judgement and innovation, he also makes stereotyped motions and is an energy source. It might be hypothesised that workers would find more interesting, and be more satisfied by, jobs which were high in their informational, judgemental and innovative inputs.

There is a link between this type of analysis and those which social psychologists and sociologists have traditionally used. Blauner assembled evidence to test his hypothesis about the importance of feelings of 'powerlessness', which he related to the extent to which a worker controlled his own pace of work, the degree of pressure exerted upon him by the process, his freedom to move about on the job, to control the quantity and quality of his production and to make choices about the techniques to be used.[1] Walker and Guest, in one of the first studies of the assembly-line worker in the automobile industry, noted those features of the job which their sample said they liked or disliked. They then ranked jobs on a three point scale for each of six such features which were: degree of repetitiveness, of mechanical pacing, skill as measured by length of learning time, frequency of breaks in routine, frequency of social intercourse and the size of the interacting group.[2]

Basing themselves on the Walker and Guest approach, another more systematic analysis of work tasks was made by Turner and Lawrence who set out—

> "to develop and implement a method of measuring job attributes that would help predict workers' response to their jobs across a wide range of differing technologies."[3]

They examined 47 jobs in a large number of industries. By observation they scored these jobs high or low in relation to selected attributes. These included variety in the number of parts, tools or controls to be manipulated or in the pace of work; autonomy in the selection of work method, sequence or pace of work; variation in the amount and kind of social interaction of either an optional or required kind; variation in the amount of responsibility measured by such things as the time taken to learn a job, or the probability of serious

1 R. Blauner, 1964, op.cit., p.21–22.
2 C. R. Walker and R. H. Guest, *The Man on the Assembly Line,* Harvard University Press, Cambridge, 1952, p.118.
3 A. N. Turner and Paul Lawrence, *"Industrial Jobs and the Worker",* Harvard University Press, Boston, 1965., p.9.

consequences of error. These concepts of autonomy in the selection of work methods and variation in the amount of responsibility are closely related to Brown's concepts of response to variability which involves a high degree of information processing and monitoring. Turner and Lawrence combined their scores of the individual attributes of their 47 jobs to produce a single overall measure which they called the "Requisite Task Attribute Score". This could then be related both to workers' perceptions of what their jobs required of them, as well as to their satisfaction with their jobs.[1]

Nothing so systematic could be attempted at Seagrass. But one of the research workers spent a period on site observing jobs in detail in the works and produced a four-fold classification which contained elements of both the Brown and the Turner and Lawrence approach. The categorisation aimed to produce groups of jobs relatively homogeneous in the extent to which they required informational or energy input, in the amount of variety provided or responsibility required.[2] The company's own job description and works number was available for each member of the original sample. Thus it was possible to allocate most of the sample to one of four categories or 'job groups' and then to re-analyse the answers to the attitude questions. The titles allocated to the job groups were (1) chemical process group, (2) the machine operation group, (3) the materials handling group and (4) the services group.

The chemical process jobs might be said to be typical of continuous flow process production, the machine operation group to be typical of mass or batch production; while the other two—materials handling and services—occur in some degree with most technologies, being supportive of the main production process.

A description of the job groups

The jobs in the "chemical process group" required little from their occupants as an energy source, but a good deal of ability to respond to environmental information, and some exercise of judgment. Men were controlling and regulating a system rather than operating a machine. Physical effort was required for a few tasks, for instance to turn heavy valves in order to transfer chemicals from one vat to another, but most of the tasks entailed the watching of panels, the recording of readings and the taking of appropriate action in response to these readings. The men doing these jobs usually had

---

1 A. N. Turner and Paul Lawrence, 1965, op. cit. p.26.
2 By 'job' we henceforth refer to the collection of activities which an individual worker was required to perform by virtue of occupying a particular position in the works. By 'task' we refer to the elements which, when combined, make up a 'job'.

considerable freedom of movement. The jobs would rate high on Turner and Lawrence's variety and autonomy scores.

The jobs in the machine operation group involved dealing with solid products and working with specific and distinct machines. Still rather little physical effort was required of the workers but most jobs involved stereo-typed and repetitive movements which demanded a good deal of surface attention and some motor skills and manual dexterity. The task elements were limited in variety. Altogether the jobs would score low on most aspects of variety and autonomy.

The jobs in the "materials handling group" involved dealing with the finished products before they left the plants. They ranged from the operation of fairly simple machinery, such as baling and bagging machines, to moving the packed product with the aid of fork lift trucks, trolleys, etc. Although mostly requiring stereotyped motions, there was more variety and autonomy than among the machine operation jobs on matters like pace of work or variety of tasks making up a job. On the other hand, they required more physical effort and very little judgement.

The jobs in the "services group" were peripheral to, but supportive of, the main production process. This group was the most heterogeneous of the four. It included work done by the tradesmen's mates, by laboratory testers and by riggers and slingers, all of whom provided ancillary services of widely differing kinds. The jobs varied in complexity. The mates were working with trades-men and their tasks could vary, both according to their own skill and their relationship with the tradesmen with whom they worked. On the whole, however, there was a good deal of variety in the mates' tasks, which required stereotyped motion, and some response to environmental information. The laboratory testers collected samples and recorded the results of tests. These workers were required to be an energy source, to make stereotyped motions and to respond to environmental information. The men in all of these jobs in the "services group" were not only free, but were required to move around the plant. They would rank high on almost all aspects of Turner and Lawrence's variety and autonomy scores.

In the analysis of the survey data a two-way classification of attitudes, by job group, within the three Works A, B and C would have been desirable. But this would have yielded very small numbers in each cell. The analysis was therefore initially carried out by using the total sample of general workers and by combining all five works together.[1] This yielded 94 cases in the

1 The total sample of general workers numbered 287 (see Table 3.1). In the present analysis 40 men not employed in any of the five main production works (the category 'other' in Table 3.1) and 20 tea makers, floor sweepers, etc. were omitted, leaving a sample size of 227.

chemical process group, 45 in the machine operation group, 28 in the materials handling group and 60 in the services group. We were not simply repeating a Works analysis because only one third of the chemical process operators came from Works A, and the remainder were distributed fairly evenly among the other four works. Half of the machine operation group came from Works C, and a little under half of the materials handling group from Works B. The services group was evenly distributed between all five works (Table 4.1).

Table 4.1   The sample of Job Groups by Works

	Works			Other	Total
	A	B	C		
Numbers in the Sample in:*					
Chemical Process	35	20	7	32	94
Machine Operation	–	4	23	18	45
Materials Handling	1	12	6	9	28
Services	16	13	11	20	60

* See footnote p.68.

When the sample of general workers had been classified in this way, a first analysis of the replies to the questions described in Chapter 3 was carried out.[1] It would have been desirable to supplement the attitude data with information about behaviour. Unfortunately it proved too big an undertaking to extract information from the company's records about absenteeism or turnover rates for individuals in these job groups. But it is worth noting that of the unofficial industrial disputes discussed in Chapter 3, one affected the chemical process group, two the materials handling group, two the services group, but five involved the machine operation group.

---

1 The precise wording of the questions has been given in Chapter 3 and will not be repeated here.

Attitudes among the job groups

General attitudes to good and bad aspects of the company as an employer
were similar for men in each of the four job groups. The good things were

Table 4.2   Unprompted answers to the question "What are some
of the things you like best about working for
(name of company)?" (by job groups). [1]

Answers*	Chemical process	Machine operation	Materials handling	Services
			Percentages	
Job security	31	31	25	33
Good amenities and facilities	22	22	25	17
Good welfare schemes, sick pay, pensions, etc.	29	38	29	28
Good working conditions	24	24	43	25
Good money	12	13	7	3
An interesting job	14	2	7	7

[1] The number of cases in the four groups in tables 4.1 to 4.6 are
chemical process 94, machine operation 45, materials handling
28 and services 60.
 * More than one answer could be given so the answers may total
more than 100 per cent.

said to be the security of employment, the good physical working conditions,
the fringe benefits and welfare amenities (Table 4.2). But the machine
operation group emerged as far more crital than the other three in its
attitudes to management worker relations in general and on the question of
whether they saw enough of management (Table 4.3). This group was also
less likely than the other three to take a "cooperational" view of the firm.

Table 4.3   "Do you think the relationship between management and workers could be improved or not?"

Answers	Chemical process	Machine operation Percentages	Materials handling	Service
Yes	58	76	50	67
No	32	15	40	22
Don't know	11	9	10	10
Total:	100	100	100	100

Only 56 per cent thought that a firm was like a football side compared with more than three quarters in both the services and the chemical process group and 68 per cent in the materials handling group (Table 4.4).

Table 4.4   "Here are two views about industry generally. I'd like you to tell me which you agree with more. Some people say that a firm is like a football side—because team work means success and is to everyone's advantage. Others say that team work in industry is impossible—because employers and men are really on opposite sides. Which view do you agree with more?" (by job groups).

Answers	Chemical process	Machine operation Percentages	Materials handling	Service
Football team	76	56	68	78
Opposite sides	16	36	25	15
Not answered/ Don't know	7	8	8	6
Total:	100	100	100	100

Clear differences also emerged in the area of pay. The median earnings of the machine operation group were highest. Eighteen per cent of them were earning £25 a week or more, compared with only 2 per cent of the chemical process group. The services group received the most widely dispersed earnings, probably reflecting the heterogeneity of jobs within this classification. Ten per cent were earning less than £15 a week and 18 per cent more than £25 (Table 4.5). Not unexpectedly then, the machine operation

Table 4.5   Previous week's gross earnings (by job groups).

Answers	Chemical process	Machine operation	Materials handling	Services
		Percentages		
Up to £15	5	2	4	10
£15 up to £17	2	7	4	13
£17 up to £20	59	38	46	38
£20 up to £25	31	36	43	18
£25 and over	2	18	4	18
Don't know	1	–	–	–
Total:	100	100	100	100

group were the most satisfied with their pay. Only 37 per cent described it as unreasonable compared with 45 to 53 per cent of the other groups. It was the chemical process group, however, who were more likely than the others to say that there were no firms in the district where they could earn more. This might have reflected a feeling that any expertise they had acquired would not be easily transferable to other employers.

The widest differences of attitude between the groups were found, as they had been when attitudes were analysed by works, in the replies to questions about job interest and supervision. The machine operation group were the most likely to describe their jobs as boring. Well over a third said the work was positively boring compared with no more than 18 per cent in any of the other groups. Only 16 per cent described it as interesting compared with 58 per cent in the chemical process group (Table 4.6). Only 13 per cent of the machine operation group felt they ever had a chance to try out their own ideas compared with 34 per cent of the chemical process and services group (Table 4.7).

Table 4.6   "Generally speaking, do you find your job is interesting, about average, or boring?" (by job groups).

Answers	Chemical process	Machine operation	Materials handling	Services
			Percentages	
Interesting	58	16	39	48
About average	18	38	36	22
Boring	13	38	18	15
It varies	11	9	8	15
Total:	100	100	100	100

Table 4.7   "Does your job give you a chance to try out ideas of your own?" (by job group).

Answers	Chemical process	Machine operation	Materials handling	Services
			Percentages	
Yes or 'sometimes'	34	13	26	35
Rarely	20	22	33	12
Never	46	64	40	54
Total:	100	100	100	100

On attitudes to supervison the dichotomy between the chemical process workers and the machine operation group was most marked. Not only did 70 per cent of the chemical process group describe their supervisors as having enough authority (Table 4.8), but two thirds got on very well with their supervisors (Table 4.9) and 40 per cent thought the right men were selected for supervisory positions. The services and materials handling group were

73

Table 4.8.   "Does your immediate superior have enough authority to answer your questions and deal with your problems?" (by job groups).

Answers	Chemical process	Machine operation	Materials handling	Services
			Percentages	
Yes	70	53	68	65
No	22	40	25	28
It varies	8	2	4	3
Don't know	1	4	4	3
Total:	100	100	100	100

Table 4.9.   "Would you say you get on with your immediate superior very well, reasonably well, or not too well?" (by job groups).

Answers	Chemical process	Machine operation	Materials handling	Services
			Percentages	
Very well	65	38	50	68
Reasonably well	31	56	32	22
Not too well	4	–	7	2
Poorly	–	6	7	–
Not answered/ don't know	–	2	4	9
Total:	100	100	100	100

quite close to the chemical process group in their attitudes towards supervision. But only a half of the machine operation group thought their supervisors had enough authority and only 38 per cent said that they got on very well with them.

The big contrast between the attitudes of the chemical process and the services group, on the one hand, and the machine operation group on the other, was consistent with the findings of writers like Blauner and Walker and Guest who had indicated that there was a positive association between satisfaction with work and the degree of variety, autonomy and discretion it offered. But earlier evidence had not all been one way. Turner and Lawrence could find no significant positive relationship between their 'job satisfaction' scores and the 'Requisite Task Attribute' scores for their total sample of jobs.[1] Only when the jobs were divided according to the size of the urban area in which they were located did a positive association emerge for those located in the smaller urban areas. This town and city dichotomy was linked with important cultural differences of religion and ethnic background, and it was at this point that Turner and Lawrence drew attention to the possible importance of influences outside of the work situation and spoke of "quite different predisposition or 'response sets' in relation to work experience".[2]

From the point of view of the present study, however, the important difference is that Turner and Lawrence's 'job satisfaction' score was compiled from replies to questions of a very general kind which almost certainly reflected an amalgam of attitudes to many aspects of the work situation like pay and quality of management as well as to the task itself. 'Job interest' in the Seagrass study, however, was a much narrower concept referring specifically to the way in which the workers rated the appeal of the work itself.

One finding of Turner and Lawrence which assumed considerable significance in the light of the Seagrass material was a negative correlation between the 'Requisite Task Attribute' scores of their jobs and absentee records of people who held those jobs.[3] For it was in the Seagrass works containing the highest proportion of the machine operation group, with the lowest amount of recorded job interest, that absenteeism was highest. On the other hand Turner and Lawrence found little correlation between satisfaction with foremen and the 'Requisite Task Attribute' score.[4] In the light of the strong association between job interest and satisfaction with supervision at Seagrass which emerged both for individual Works and for the job groups this appeared puzzling. However, the Turner and Lawrence material contained some curious divergencies when the individual components of the task attribute score were examined. Thus it appeared that men in jobs where task

---

1   A. N. Turner and Paul Lawrence, 1965, op. cit. p.49–68.
2   Ibid., p.90.
3   See also A. H. Brayfield and W. H. Crockett, 1955, op. cit.
4   A. N. Turner and Paul Lawrence, 1965, op. cit., p.65.

variety was low were more satisfied with supervision, but so, too, were men in jobs where 'task identity' (in brief, where the worker could see what he was contributing to the total process) was high. This suggested that the causal connection between the characteristics of the work task, or job, and the attitudes to or perception of supervison by workers performing that job, was an area which required further study. It is a point to which we shall return when we discuss our own examination of the influences of the managerial control systems in use, upon the relationship between supervisor and supervised.[1]

Attitudes within the chemical process and machine operation groups

In the case of the chemical process and the machine operation group we felt that the numbers, although small, might sustain a further analysis. The chemical process workers in Works A could be compared with the remainder of the chemical process group and the machine operation workers in Works C with the remainder of that group. The analysis was confined to the areas of job interest, attitudes to supervision and to management where the largest differences by Works and by job group had already been found.

Immediately a pattern of greater satisfaction emerged from the Works A chemical process workers. They had a consistently higher degree of job interest than the other chemical process workers. Three quarters of them, compared with less than half of the others, found their job interesting and only 3 per cent described it as boring compared with 19 per cent of the rest. Only 18 per cent of the Works A men, compared with as many as 63 per cent of the remainder, felt that the job never gave them enough opportunity to try out their own ideas. They were also consistently more enthusiastic about their immediate supervision. For instance, 44 per cent of them, compared with only 15 per cent of the remainder described their supervision as *very* adequate; over a half compared with less than a third of the rest were prepared to say that the "right" men were chosen as supervisors and 74 per cent compared with 59 per cent got on with their supervisors very well. Eighty-two per cent of the Works A chemical process group compared with 72 per cent of the remainder said a firm was like a football team (Table 4.10).

The difference between Works C and the rest of the machine operation group in the area of job interest and supervision was not nearly so marked nor so uniform. If anything the Works C men in this group expressed a marginally more favourable attitude to the job itself than the others. For instance 35 per cent of Works C men in the machine operation group compared with 41 per

---

1   See Chapter 7.

Table 4.10 A comparison of selected attitudes of Works A and the remainder of the chemical process group.[1]

	Works A	Remainder
	Percentages	
Job interesting?[2]	76	47
About average	15	20
Boring	3	19
It varies	6	14
Can you try out ideas?		
Yes	32	17
Sometimes	15	8
Rarely	35	12
Never	18	63
Is your supervision:		
Very adequate	44	15
Adequate	41	63
Not very adequate	6	5
Inadequate	6	10
Varies	3	2
Don't know	–	5
Does the company choose the right men as supervisors?		
Yes	56	30
Sometimes only	18	20
No	21	42
Don't know	6	7
Do you get on well with your immediate superior?		
Very well	74	59
Reasonably well	24	36
Other answers	3	5
Firm is like a football team		
Football team	82	72
Opposite sides	15	17
Not answered/don't know	3	10

1 There were 34 cases in Works A and 59 in the remainder.
2 The precise wording of the questions may be found in the corresponding tables, Chapter 3.

Table 4.11   A comparison of selected attitudes of Works C. and
the remainder of the machine operation group.[1]

	Works C.	Remainder
	Percentages	
Job interesting?[2]	17	14
About average	35	41
Boring	35	41
It varies	13	5
Can you try out ideas?		
Yes	13	5
Sometimes	4	5
Rarely	26	18
Never	57	73
Is your supervision		
Very adequate	9	9
Adequate	65	64
Not very adequate	9	5
Inadequate	17	9
Varies	–	5
Don't know	–	9
Does the company choose the right men as supervisors?		
Yes	17	23
Sometimes only	30	23
No	52	45
Don't know	–	9
Do you get on well with your immediate superior?		
Very well	43	32
Reasonably well	48	64
Other answers	8	5
Firm is like a football team		
Football team	48	64
Opposite sides	43	27
Not answered/don't know	8	9

[1] There were 23 cases in Works C and 22 in the remainder.
[2] The precise wording of the questions may be found in the
corresponding tables, Chapter 3.

cent of the remainder described their job as boring and more of them said that it varied. Only 57 per cent in Works C compared with 73 per cent of the remainder said that they could never try out their own ideas and fewer, too, said that they did not have enough freedom. Attitudes to supervision were not all that dissimilar. Works C machine operation men were more likely than the others to say that they got on well with their supervisor in personal terms and were as likely to describe their supervision as *very* adequate or adequate. On the other hand they were more likely to argue that the selection of supervisors was faulty. Perhaps the most marked difference, however, lay in the proportions who took a cooperational view of the firm. Only 48 per cent of the Works C machine operation group chose the teamwork analogy compared with 64 per cent of the remainder (Table 4.11).

To summarise, it appeared that at Seagrass, workers in jobs which provided a good deal of freedom to choose their pace of working, to choose the sequence in which tasks were carried out and which provided an opportunity to move about the plant physically as well as to engage in a variety of tasks, were more likely to describe those jobs as interesting. More surprising, perhaps, they were also more likely to display favourable attitudes towards supervision. This suggests that the general workers did vary considerably in their experience of the production system and that the impact of technology might be thought of as operating primarily through what has been called the 'man-machine' system, that is through the way in which the actual work tasks themselves were shaped by the production system. On the other hand the differences between chemical process workers in Works A and in other Works suggested that this might not be the whole of the story. One possibility, however, which had to be allowed for first was that the job groups were too crude, and that the original classification had placed together jobs which, after all, were significantly different in degrees of autonomy, pacing, etc. Thus it was that the research workers returned to the site for a further and more detailed study of a few specific jobs in the three works A, B and C.

Description of particular jobs in Works A, B and C

The chemical process operators in Works A were engaged in the kind of activity which represented the paradigm of automation. The control room of one of the Works A plants resembled the workplace of the future. Some writers have suggested that automation will remove all interest from work because the monitoring of dials is a boring activity. Blauner had already challenged this argument on the ground that automation confers a great sense of responsibility upon the operator and that the individual worker obtains a sense of control.[1] Against this background it was interesting to examine precisely what the process operator on Works A did and to consider whether there was any reason for him to find his job more interesting than his opposite number on Works B or C.

The Works A operator's task of reading dials, recording observations and making suitable adjustments has already been described in general. On that Works the operator had some discretion as to when, and in which sequence, these tasks were carried out. Moreover when all was going well and there was no breakdown he had great freedom to vary the pace of work, and to move about, or even to chat. As one assistant foreman said, "That's one thing about working here, you're not tied to the job like on an assembly line—a man can take a smoke or a break if he wants it". On the other hand, if something was not running smoothly and well, he would probably be involved in an urgent discussion with his foreman, or even his plant manager, about what corrective action should be taken. As we have seen the process workers felt that "on big upsets the management muck in with you at once".[2] But because in Works A the product did not change and the plants could run continuously for long periods of time there was an opportunity for the workers to develop their own routine and pacing. All men on Works A were trained to do two or three jobs so that continuous operation could be ensured in case of sickness, accident or holidays. They could also train for higher category jobs carrying more responsibility. A few exceptional operators would know as many as twelve jobs. This enabled the men to understand how their work fitted in with that of other people, which probably contributed to their belief in teamwork. It also offered prospects of betterment within the limits of the job category system on the Seagrass site.

The chemical process operators in Works A had a sense of responsibility for the maintenance of the process. They also appeared more conscious of their identity as chemical workers than the men on other works. They were interested in the idea of a chemical workers' union because, as they put it, "each 'trade' should have its own union". They also empahsised the importance of adequate training for the job, which suggested that they took pride in their technical competence.

In what way, if any, did chemical operators' tasks on Works B and C differ? The actual work of monitoring and recording was the same, and there were also possibilities of promotion to more responsible higher category jobs. But in both Works B and C the chemical operators had less discretion to vary the time or the pace at which they carried out their task and they also had less freedom of movement. In Works B the chemical process itself was more

---

1 R. Blauner 1964, op.cit., p.172—173.
2 See Chapter 3, p.44.

complex than in Works A. It could go off line and cause major trouble in micro-seconds. So the operators were required to give it constant attention and to respond immediately to any sign of anything going wrong. Increasing automation was also demanding greater vigilance.[1]

On Works B and C, the frequent changes of variety also resulted in less freedom for the operator. A changeover on a plant in Works B might mean the operators moving temporarily to a train in another part of the plant. This prevented them from developing a regular routine and rhythm of work. Furthermore the supervisors had to keep track of them. On Works C the chemical process was even less fully automated than on either Works A or B and the operator had to transfer materials semi-manually and at specific times and these varied according to the nature of the particular variety of the product. Thus the operator's discretion to change the order in which he carried out tasks, his freedom of movement and his ability to develop a regular rhythm were restricted on both Works B and C.

In many ways the chemical process operators on Works B and C appeared less well off for freedom and the exercise of discretion than the majority of the "services group" who were called upon to travel all over the plants and in some cases, even, the Works. The jobs of laboratory testers or tradesmen's mates offered considerable opportunity for diverse social interaction when taking samples or when discussing the nature of the repair or maintenance job to be carried out. These jobs also gave their occupants a considerable sense of responsibility and they were called upon to exercise judgement within limits. This did not always result in increased satisfaction, however, because it could raise expectations. The mates, for instance, compared their own knowledge and competence favourably with that of the tradesmen whom they assisted and felt their own expertise received insufficient recognition. In general, however, the workers in the services group were in jobs which they could see as essential to the smooth operation of the whole process, and from this they derived a good deal of satisfaction, whichever Works they were employed upon.

It is interesting to note, however, the variety of ways in which freedom of movement and opportunities for social interaction may be provided in the work situation. A good illustration is provided by a comparison of the situation of the materials handling group in the warehouse of Works B, and of the filament yarn inspectors, also materials handling, in Works C. The work in the warehouse was unautomated at the time of our survey and was completely routine and unskilled. Men filled, sewed and palleted sacks of the product on moving conveyor belts. They controlled the pace of their work

---

1 See Chapter 6, p.114.

but only within the limits set by the belt, and they could not vary the way or order in which the tasks were performed. It was a typical conveyor belt situation with stereotyped motions to be performed. It was, however, possible to relieve the monotony by stopping the lines completely from time to time so that all the men on a shift could take a smoke or a meal break together. In this sense, therefore, there was some freedom.

Work in the inspection department in Works C was also extremely routine. Each bobbin of yarn had to be held up to a bright light to search for flaws, then weighed to check that it was the correct size, wrapped in tissue paper and finally packed in a box. Talking on the job was impossible because each man was sitting in a partly enclosed cubicle, cut off from his workmates. He repeated the sequence of operations over and over again. The operators developed a special skill which enabled them to detect flaws unnoticeable even to other experienced men and they were proud of this. But it was a limited skill. They could also build up banks of work. This enabled them, within limits, to start late and finish early or to vary their pace of work from time to time. On this job, too, the men could stop work together for breaks.

Without doubt the jobs which scored lowest on almost all elements, including lack of variety and autonomy, were to be found among the machine operation group in the staple fibre and filament yarn areas of Works C. In the staple fibre area the extruded molten polymer was passed continuously through a series of machines which stretched, crimped, dyed and finally chopped and baled the yarn. In the spinning area there were three basic jobs—that of the pack operator who handled the polymer, of the spinner and of the doffer. Some variety had been introduced by rotating the men between the three tasks, so that each spent four weeks spinning, two weeks doffing and one week as pack operator. Incidentally this meant a higher job category for the men in this section because they could do three jobs. But beyond this there was no prospect of promotion to any higher category jobs. The men worked as a team and there was some social interaction on the job. On the other hand, the machines were running continuously except when the variety of the product was changed, or there was a breakdown. They could not be left untended, although a small degree of flexibility was obtained because the pack operator could build up a reserve which enabled him to relieve other members of the team occasionally.

The processing side of the staple fibre area was similar, except that here the three main jobs of baler operator, cutter operator and draw frame operator were not rotated. They represented a limited hierarchy of jobs of increasing skill, so that men could be promoted from one job category to another higher one.

82

Freedom to interact socially, to move about and to vary the pace of work was lowest of all in the filament yarn area of Works C. Close attention to the routine operation of machine minding was required the whole time to maintain the quality of the product in both the spinning and draw-twist areas. For example, if one of the holes in the spinaret was feeding through an irregular thickness the operator had to detect this immeditely otherwise the fault might not be discovered again until the yarns came to be knitted or dyed, that is after they had been sold to the customer. The pace of work of the spinner was dictated completely by the pace of the machine and the varying nature of the product, for example finer or coarser yarn. He patrolled his machine doffing the bobbins at a precisely defined time to give the correct weight. He was isolated with his machine from other operators and had to be constantly on the alert for mishaps. Once he had become a trained spinner there was no higher category job for him to be promoted to.

The work in the draw twist area had similar disadvantages. There was no freedom of movement. It was necessary to be constantly on the alert for breaks in the yarn and to doff and restring the bobbin. The draw-twist area was made up of a number of rooms in each of which about 40 men were working. The quality and type of machine varied between the rooms and at the time of our survey, the operators rotated in order to even out the opportunities for working on the better machines or better qualities of yarn. This meant that the men did not necessarily know who would take over from them at the end of the shift. In this situation it was easy to succumb to the temptation of doffing the bobbins early. The next bobbin then became over-full and jammed the machine at the beginning of the next shift which caused frustration to the operator taking over. No rotation of jobs was possible in the draw-twist area and there were no higher category jobs for promotion.

Thus although jobs could be said to share certain general characteristics in that they could be placed together upon a crude continuum which scored variety, autonomy, pacing, etc, a further analysis would suggest that the jobs giving greatest satisfaction to the general workers at Seagrass would be those of the Works A chemical process jobs, and those giving lowest would be the machine operation jobs on Works C.

Physical working conditions

So far we have not taken account of the physical working environment. Seagrass general workers and tradesmen alike considered working conditions to be one of the most important factors to be taken into account when judging the attractiveness of jobs in general.[1] It came second only to pay in

---

1 See Chapter 5, p.96.

the frequency with which it was mentioned. At the same time the sample expressed general satisfaction with the working conditions found at Seagrass. It was one of the four most frequently mentioned good aspects of working for the company.[1] Favourable comparisons were made with previous experiences in the construction and iron and steel industries. Nevertheless there were considerable variations in the attractiveness of the working conditions in different works on the Seagrass site and in reply to a direct question, general workers in Works A showed themselves to be the most satisfied, followed by those in Works B and finally those in Works C. Among those who were critical, the Works C men were the most likely to make concrete suggestions for improvement.

Chemical process operators, wherever they were, tended to work in some of the cleanest, coolest and quietest areas. But undoubtedly the most pleasant conditions were to be found in Works A. It was not that different works had different standards but rather, the nature of the chemical process on Works B and C was such that it produced more heat and noise. In Works B too, there was the disruption caused by the ongoing technical changes. Similarly while most machine operation workers were involved in work situations where there was more noise than most chemical process operators, the machine operation workers on Works C, and in particular the spinning and draw twist operators in the filament yarn section, had the most unpleasant working conditions. The work surroundings were clean, but the atmosphere was humid and the noise of the machines made communication extremely difficult. These variations in physical working conditions were of such a kind, therefore, that they too could have contributed to the satisfaction on Works A and to the discontent on Works C.

The accident risk varied between the Works. The danger arising from the handling of highly inflammable materials was considerable in both Works A and B. But the workers seemed to take this for granted. Men on all three Works were alike in that the majority believed management to be sincere in its concern for accident prevention, and alike in attributing a recent rise in the accident rate to the workers themselves, particularly to new recruits. But if a parallel could be drawn with other high risk industries, like mining, it could well be that the awareness of danger contributed to the teamwork spirit which was found to be higher in Works A and B than in Works C.[2]

---

1 See Chapter 3, p.35.
2 See Chapter 3, p.42–43.

Summary

The classification of jobs into the four groups—chemical process, machine operation, materials handling and services—had been on the basis of an assessment of broad variations in energy and informational inputs, the amount of variety provided or responsibility required. The chemical process and machine operation jobs, which we subjected to the closest analysis, were typically associated with two broad types of core technology, that is continuous flow process production and mass or large batch production. The services and materials handling group were supportive of the main production process.

Attitudes of workers were quite clearly differentiated between the job groups in two broad areas, the interest of the work and feelings about supervision. These were also the main areas of difference between the Works. One conclusion might then be that Works' differences were simply a reflection of the different composition of jobs on the Works, and that the main link between technology and workers' attitudes was through the influence of technology on the nature of the work task in the sense discussed in this chapter i.e. the man-machine system. Works A jobs were almost entirely in the chemical process and services groups with the most favourable attitudes to the job itself and to supervision. Works C jobs were heavily concentrated on the machine operation group with unfavourable attitudes to the job and to supervision. Finally, Works B contained a variety of jobs from each of the four groups and this might explain, why in the examination of attitudes by Works, it had fallen between the extremes of Works A and C.

There was, however, one interesting discovery. The chemical process operators on Works A were far more enthusiastic about their work and supervision than the remainder of the process operators on the site. On the other hand, the machine operation group on Works C were more critical in some respects than the rest of this group on the site. The explanation seemed at least in part to be that there were important differences in the characteristics of the jobs within these groups which our classification had obscured. These differences were in turn associated with differences in certain broad characteristics of the technology, for example, differences in the nature of the chemistry, in the number of varieties of product, and in the way in which quality was controlled. These aspects of the production task all had a significant influence upon the amount of discretion the operator could exercise and upon the variety in the job.

But did this rule out entirely the possibility that there was a "Works effect" superimposed upon the effect of differences of job content? Was it not possible that a heavy concentration of workers in jobs which they found relatively satisfying might have a cumulative effect in producing a happy atmosphere in Works A and vice versa in Works C? Perhaps, more importantly, the job classification only took account very indirectly of the kind of social relationships which the different tasks involved. Account was taken of the ability to move around the plant or control room as a desirable feature of a job. But the job classification gave no weight, for instance, to the kind of interaction which the work task required between operators and supervisors. Yet this appeared to be an important factor because of the marked difference of attitudes to supervision. It was not entirely clear why, for instance, a lot of variety or opportunity to exercise judgement should be associated with favourable attitudes to supervision. At an intuitive level it might be argued that a worker left to exercise judgement might feel that there was less interference or control by the foreman. But there were hints in the material presented in this chapter that how far the foreman 'interfered' or had to give instructions—that is how far he fulfilled a trouble shooting or policing role—was influenced not only by the hardware, the collection of plant, tools and recipes, but also by the nature of the administrative systems devised for production scheduling, quality and cost control. Did a production situation which called for constant changes of variety, or for high standards of quality control where a number of variables had to be watched at the same time, imply a different relationship between supervisor and supervised from one where there was continuous production of one variety and where quality control was automatic? With these questions in mind, the researchers decided to return to Seagrass to examine those aspects of the control system which seemed central to the relationships of foremen and men.

Before that was done, however, there was material in the attitude survey which had not yet been explored. In the course of the interviews we had collected information about the previous work experience of the sample, about their general attitudes to work, what they looked for in work in general and about their attitude to their trade union. In Chapter 3 we implicitly assumed that we were dealing with a group of workers who were relatively homogeneous in origin. Yet the differences which emerged there between the tradesmen on the one hand, and the general workers on the other, pointed to the importance of the influence of factors located outside the immediate work situation. The tradesmen's attitudes to some aspects of Seagrass employment were intelligible only in the context of their holding norms and values which they had acquired during the period of their craft apprentice-ship. In the next chapter, therefore, we examine the general descriptive material about backgrounds and expectations for the whole sample, of both general workers and tradesmen. Our object is to see whether there were any differences of experience or of priorities in wants which could throw light on the differences of attitudes and behaviour displayed in the work situation.

5 The Workers' Backgrounds

The exploration of what might be called the 'man machine system' in the previous chapter enabled us to be more specific about the way in which the general workers' daily activities and experiences were structured by the production system, and to put forward some hypotheses about possible connections between these experiences and the responses which they evoked. The varying requirements of the jobs might be seen as constraints imposed upon workers who accepted employment at Seagrass. But their response to those constraints could, perhaps, only be fully understood in the context of the needs which they were seeking to satisfy when taking the job.[1]

It is possible to distinguish two strands in the development of the idea that workers may have differing wants and needs to be satisfied in work. The first can be called social psychological and the second sociological. Even before the work of Mayo and his associates became available, American management was beginning to question or even to reject the model of the worker as 'rational economic man' seeking to maximise his economic return.[2]

> "By the 1930's this awareness of workers as 'human beings' was widespread among American employers. Failure to treat workers as human beings came to be regarded as the cause of low morale, poor craftsmanship, unresponsiveness and confusion."

Once the results of the Hawthorne experiments were available, accompanied by Mayo's own philosophical commentary, the foundation of a new orthodoxy—'the human relations' school of management theory—was laid. The worker was seen as having economic, social and psychological needs which all had to be satisfied in work.[3] A major contribution to the conceptualization of this framework came from the work of Maslow.[4] It was

---

1 See Chapter 1, p.22.
2 R. Bendix, *Work and Authority in Industry*, Harper and Row, New York, 1963, p.294. This masterly review of the development of management ideology shows how, as early as 1923, 'progressive' management was concerned with human relations. Mayo's work fell on fertile ground.
3 For a review of the development of management's assumptions about people, see E. Schein *Organisational Psychology*, Prentice Hall, Englewood Cliffs, 1965, Chapter 4.
4 A. Maslow, *Motivation and Personality*, Harper, New York, 1954.

he who postulated a 'hierarchy' of needs; that lower order needs must be adequately satisfied before the next higher order needs could develop. 'Needs', however, were seen as innate. There has followed an enormous literature on the problems of reconciling personal and organizational needs. For the most part, however, relatively little attention has been paid to the possibility that the importance of different needs could vary as between different groups of workers. In so far as a range of needs is seen to exist, the rather simple assumption has been made that there is a linear change of needs over time i.e. that as standards of living rise so all workers gradually attach more importance to the satisfaction of their social and psychological needs. Moreover, there has been curiously little concern with the locus of satisfaction. Must all human needs be satisfied in the work situation? What of the role of family and community?

There is, however, a growing body of empirical evidence which points to important differences in the priorities attached by different groups of workers to what they seek from their employment situation. Professional and higher level white collar workers appear to place more emphasis upon the importance of having interesting work or responsibility than do manual workers. This might possibly be an example of the simple operation of the hiearchy concept. Because professionals, lower order economic needs are better satisfied, they can turn their attention to the satisfaction of other, psychological needs. Whilst this is undoubtedly part of the explanation it is also clear that the educational system creates, or at least reinforces, the expectation that professional jobs *should* be interesting. Thus students destined to occupy professional jobs often lay more emphasis upon job interest than economic reward even before they enter and have experience of the labour market.

In this respect we find the approach of what has been called the sociological stream, more convincing. Here social experience is seen as contributing to the shaping of expectations and of needs. It then follows that systematic variations in the needs of different groups develop because they are exposed to different experiences and influences. As Goldthorpe and his colleagues have expressed it:—

> "For wants and expectations are culturally determined *variables*, not psychological constants; and from a sociological standpoint what is a fact of major interest *is* the variation in the ways in which groups differently located in the social structure actually experience and attempt to meet the needs which at a different level of analysis may be attributed to them all." [1]

1   J. Goldthorpe, et. al., 1968, op. cit., p.178.

This led us to examine further our own research material. First if it was possible to discern a different ordering of wants and expectations among different groups of Seagrass workers, what kind of factors were likely to have been influential in producing these differences? They would probably include such things as the nature of the local community, the values transmitted to the worker by his family or by his general social milieu and his own experience of social mobility. Second, if it may be presumed that when workers have a choice of jobs they will select that one which most nearly satisfies their ordering of wants, how far had workers at Seagrass been able to choose their jobs and thus contribute to the formation of the particular constellations of attitudes we had found on the Works? Third, were there any systematic variations among our sample in what they said they were looking for from their job which might be related to different attitudes and behaviour.

Experiences before coming to Seagrass

Lockwood has described the kind of community structure from which what he has called the 'traditional worker' is likely to emerge.

"The isolated and endogamous nature of the community, its predominantly one-class population and low rates of geographical and social mobility all tend to make it an inward-looking society and to accentuate the sense of cohesion that springs from shared work experiences." [1]

The area in which the Seagrass workers lived possessed many of these characteristics. It was predominantly working class. The majority of the men travelled from a large northern working class town which lay on one edge of the site.[2] Some, it is true, came from smaller more mixed communities to the south and as the site developed a few housing estates had grown up around its perimeter. But again, these were mostly occupied by manual workers. Apart from Seagrass, the area, as we have noted, was heavily dependent upon two 'traditional' industries—shipbuilding and iron and steel. There were undoubtedly some signs of change. But to the extent that these gave any indication of a weakening of the uniform class character of the area, it was due to the growth of Seagrass itself. The chemical complex employed a higher proportion of technical, professional and administrative workers than the

---

1 D. Lockwood, "Sources of Variation in Working Class Images of Society", *The Sociological Review,* Vol. 14., No.3., 1966, p.251.
2 Seventy per cent of the sample lived within 5 miles of the site.

other industries in the area. But most of these white collar groups had been recruited outside and had moved into the area. In any case these were marginal changes.

The geographical mobility of our sample was extremely low. Between 70 and 80 per cent of both tradesmen and general workers had lived in the catchment area all their lives (Table 5.1). Indeed, well over a third had never moved from the immediate locality in which they were born; and less than 10 per cent had moved from further afield than other parts of Yorkshire or from Tyneside.

Table 5.1   Geographical Mobility

Answers	Tradesmen	Works A	B	C	All General Workers
		Percentages			
Has always lived in the catchment area	75	72	79	74	76
Has moved to the area from:					
Elsewhere in Yorkshire	6	11	7	4	7
Tyneside	8	6	4	6	3
North and Midlands	4	6	6	12	5
South and Wales	5	2	2	–	3
Other (inc. Ireland)	1	2	2	2	2
No information	1	2	–	2	2
Total:	100	100	100	100	100

We have no evidence about social mobility. But 90 per cent of the general workers had left school at the minimum age of 14, or in the case of the younger workers, 15. One small difference between the Works was that 12 per cent of the Works C general workers had left school at 16 or later, compared with only 6 per cent in Works A. The group most likely to have stayed on at school, however, were the tradesmen among whom nearly a fifth had

90

remained until 16 or later. Over a quarter of the tradesmen were time-served Seagrass men. But only 16 per cent were without any other employment experience; the majority of those who had served their apprenticeship at Seagrass had taken a job elsewhere but had then subsequently returned to the company.

All of the general workers' jobs at Seagrass would be characterised as semi-skilled by the Registrar General's occupational classification. It was interesting to find, therefore, that quite a number of men had worked either as skilled craftsmen or in white collar or supervisory positions before coming to Seagrass. The percentage with white collar or craft backgrounds was largest in Works B and C (about a third) and lowest in Works A (just over a fifth).

Table 5.2   Industry of employment before Seagrass

Industry of last employment	Tradesmen	Works A	B	C	All General Workers
		Percentages			
Iron and Steel	19	30	26	33	33
Shipbuilding	9	4	2	–	3
Construction	12	6	24	12	14
Chemical	7	4	7	6	5
Service	11	4	7	4	6
Other Manufacturing	7	9	13	14	10
All other Industries [1]	7	32	15	20	21
Armed Forces (inc. Merchant Navy)	12	11	6	12	8
No other job [2]	16	–	–	–	–
Total:	100	100	100	100	100

[1] Includes mining, agriculture, public utilities, transport and communication.
[2] Tradesmen who served their apprenticeship at Seagrass and stayed.

The industrial background of the sample reflected the economy of the area. A third of the general workers had moved from the iron and steel industry, and another sizeable group had been recruited from construction (Table 5.2). The way in which the make-up of the labour force of a particular Works could vary in a fairly random way, is illustrated by the fact that a slack period for the construction industry in the area had coincided with one of the periods of expansion and recruitment to Works B so that a quarter of the general workers in that Works had been drawn from that industry. Sizeable groups of the tradesmen had been employed in the iron and steel, ship-building, construction and service industries, before coming to Seagrass.

Since the Seagrass site had only been in operation for seventeen years it was perhaps not surprising to find that the workers were rather young (Table 5.3). Only 26 per cent of our total sample (general workers and tradesmen) were over 45 compared with 42 per cent of men in the chemical industry in the country as a whole. The tradesmen, as might be expected from the

Table 5.3   Age Distribution

Age Group	Tradesmen	Works A	B	C	All General Workers
		Percentages			
21–25	24	6	11	14	11
26–30	12	11	17	22	18
31–35	10	17	17	6	11
36–40	19	13	7	18	14
41–45	20	21	19	12	14
46–50	7	11	13	10	11
51–55	6	13	13	16	12
56–60	2	6	4	4	7
60 and over	–	2	–	–	2
Total:	100	100	100	100	100

numbers who had served their apprenticeship at Seagrass, were younger than the site average. Nearly a quarter of them were between 21 and 25 compared with 11 per cent of general workers. The percentage of general workers in each of the three Works over the age of 45 was the same, about 30 per cent, but of tradesmen only 15 per cent. There was a considerable difference in the proportions within the younger age groups among the general workers. Works C had almost twice as many workers between the ages of 21 and 30 as did Works A. As we shall see later this was the result of a deliberate selection policy by Works C management.

The great majority of the sample were married, 85 per cent of the tradesmen and 90 per cent of the general workers, but the age differences described above were reflected in the kind of families the men had. More tradesmen, and more of the general workers in Works C, had dependent children. Home ownership was generally high among the sample. Nearly a half were buying or owned their own homes compared with a national figure of 35 per cent in households where the head was a manual worker.[1] But the percentage of general workers buying a house with a mortgage was rather higher among the Works C men than the other two Works. Most of those renting occupied council houses.

Although the differences between the Works were small it did appear that the Works C general workers might have heavier financial commitments with their mortgages and their young families to support. If this were so, it would not be surprising if they were particularly sensitive not only to absolute levels of pay, but also to any fluctuations from week to week as a result of bonus variations.

Methods of Recruitment to Seagrass

There was one very important difference between the tradesmen and the general workers. The tradesmen had made a conscious decision, at a fairly early age, to commit themselves to a specific occupation and to undergo a four or five year apprenticeship at relatively low rates of pay and they were then recruited to Seagrass specifically as fitters, electricians, etc.

Very few of the general workers, on the other hand, could have had much idea of what work on the site was like, although they had probably talked about it. It seemed from some preliminary enquiries we made, that family and friends were important influences in drawing attention to the possibility of jobs at Seagrass. But, at least until the early sixties, the relatively high rate of unemployment and the lack of industrial development made the choice of jobs in the area very limited. There was little opportunity therefore for men to

1 *Family Expenditure Survey, 1966*, H.M.S.O., London, 1967, Table 9.

engage in any very sophisticated matching of job opportunities against their own needs.

The tradesmen and the general workers were alike in their reasons for leaving the job they held before Seagrass. There was one group who had lost their previous job or had finished National Service and therefore *had* to find a job. Another group of about the same size wanted to change jobs for health reasons. A third group were looking for better pay and the fourth for more security.

When asked why they had taken the Seagrass job the security offered was by far the most important reason (Table 5.4). It was stressed slightly more, perhaps, by general workers than by tradesmen, but certainly no less by Works A general workers than by Works C.

Table 5.4   Unprompted answers to the question "Why did you decide to join (name of company) in the first place?"

Answers*	Tradesmen	Works			All General Workers
		A	B	C	
			Percentages		
Security	30	42	39	43	42
"A good firm to work for"	25	17	11	26	15
Good or better money	18	21	22	14	19
Good or better prospects	12	21	17	22	20
"It was a job"	17	25	22	14	17
Interest of the job	13	4	2	6	4
Because of family or friends	8	6	11	4	5
Proximity to home	8	4	13	6	5
Other	15	17	15	12	12

* More than one answer could be given so the answers may total to more than 100 per cent

"Heard a lot about it like—offers you security—not afraid to be off sick." (General worker, Works B)

"(Seagrass) offered security—also pension, share scheme—didn't have any of these in the steel works." (General worker, Works A)

"For the area—it was the security I was after—with a wife and family you want security." (General worker, Works C)

Money, prospects and the general reputation of the company, (which was also related to the regularity of employment because this was one of the reasons for regarding the company highly) were all referred to as important. Only the tradesmen were significantly influenced by the interest of the work. In an area still scarred with the memories of the depression, to say nothing of lesser but sometimes worrying post war unemployment, the emphasis upon security was understandable. The impression given by these interviews was that there was very little choice of jobs in the area and that there was a very large measure of agreement among all the groups about what made the Seagrass job attractive. There was little evidence of any marked difference in the ordering of wants here. But after having decided to work at Seagrass was there any possibility that preferences for say, interesting work as against higher pay, could lead to some general workers taking jobs in Works A as compared with Works C?

Any such opportunities were limited by the Company recruitment policy. From the time the site was first developed the Company had recruited general workers through a labour "pool". From there they were then sent out to individual works. In theory, therefore, a man could not present himself at Seagrass saying "I wish to work on Works A rather than on Works C". Until about 1963 there was a buyers' market for labour and there was little pressure to deviate from this labour pool system which had the advantage for the Company of giving time to sort out the new recruits. As attracting labour became more difficult, so there was some shift towards direct recruitment to the individual Works. In the period 1960—64 for instance, an average of 20 per cent of the new recruits to Works A, 30 per cent to Works B and 45 per cent to Works C came from direct recruitment. [1] But despite this trend, the bulk of the labour force at the time we were interviewing had come via the labour pool and its common recruitment policy.

The theoretical policy of the labour pool was to send men in turn, to fill casual vacancies on the Works, or for interview for a trial for a permanent

1 The figures for Works C relate to the average of the two years 1963—4 only. Those for earlier years were not available.

vacancy. The Works had their own simple systems of selection. Thus Works C did not normally accept men over 35 for the filament yarn section because it was believed that manual dexterity decreased with age. They also looked, as they put it, for men with rather "higher levels of intelligence" for the chemical process area. Works A might test for ability to do simple decimal calculations or to calculate odds on horses, on the principle that if a man could do that, he could also read the panels in the control room. But in practice, according to management, few men had been rejected on the basis of these tests. This was borne out by the replies to a question on the labour pool which we put to our sample. Many, it seemed, thought that they had never been in the labour pool. They had arrived at Seagrass, been sent to a Works and stayed there.

We could not, of course, rule out the possiblity that there was selection, not by the men themselves, but by the foreman of the labour pool, at the point where he sent men to the various Works for interview. After all, he knew what the Works were looking for. Second, as we have seen above, there could have been, and was, some selection by the Works themselves. This probably accounted for some of the differences already found between Works A and C. The men in Works C were younger because of the emphasis upon the advantage of youth and possibly these workers more often had skilled manual or white collar backgrounds because of an emphasis upon alertness and "the kind of men we need". One final possibility of selection remained. If men whose particular needs were not satisfied in one Works had applied for transfer to other Works there might have been some congregation of men with particular priorities. But we were told that such transfers rarely occurred.

On the whole, therefore, the only evidence that can be found of non-random allocation of men to Works comes from management policy. The men themselves chose to go and work at Seagrass for remarkably similar reasons. Having arrived, which Works they finally ended up in depended upon management. This selection process did send rather younger workers and possibly rather more with white collar or craft backgrounds to Works C.

Orientations to and expectations of work

A further indication of what sort of things the sample felt were important aspects of work were supplied by the replies to a question which asked people to name "the three most important factors making a job a good one". Two replies stood out above all others. For tradesmen as well as for general workers in all three Works, money and good physical working conditions were the most important. Thus the main emphasis of the sample was upon extrinsic attributes of the job. Table 5.5 shows that a wide range of other

96

Table 5.5   Unprompted answers to the question "What do you think are the three most important factors in making a job a good one?"

Answers*	Tradesmen	Works A	B	C	All General Workers
		Percentages			
Money	61	57	48	59	54
Good working conditions i.e. amenities, a clean job	53	70	63	69	61
An interesting, varied job	27	14	11	18	16
A well-planned and organised job	18	4	7	8	5
To be on top of your job, to be able to exercise a good standard of craftsmanship	17	19	20	18	16
Good supervision	20	17	43	12	23
Good management	9	8	15	8	9
Appreciation from and communication with management	19	19	9	20	15
Good security, sick pay, and pension schemes	20	15	13	8	12
Good workmates	16	16	17	10	17
Other (including promotion prospects)	17	17	38	43	39
Don't know	22	22	17	29	33

* Each respondent was asked to name three factors. The total number of respondents naming a factor is shown as a percentage of the total number in the sample.

aspects of the work situation were mentioned after these two, and having examined the preliminary results it appeared that the tradesmen were placing more emphasis upon factors related to the performance of the job itself or what might be called job-related factors—'interest and variety', 'a well organised job', 'being on top of the job'.

Because of our interest in any emphasis upon intrinsic rewards relating to the nature of work itself, a special analysis was made which showed that more than a half of the tradesmen mentioned at least one of these job-related aspects among their 'three best things' but only one third of the general workers had done so. Typical tradesmen's comments were:—

"Most important is the job interest—that's 90 per cent of the battle." (Fitter)

"Plenty to go at—plenty of work to keep your mind occupied—e.g. materials always there for the job." (Instrument Artificer)

"The self-satisfaction that I've done a good job." (Fitter)

Emphasis upon the intrinsic rewards of work follows logically from the tradesmens' sense of their own worth as skilled men which we commented upon earlier.[1] Their work was an expression of their 'self'. Indeed it was interesting to see how frequently the tradesmen criticised their present employment in order to underline how highly they valued the opportunity to do a job well:—

"Being allowed to enjoy one's craft—enough time to do a good job—which you don't get here!" (Electrician)

"To practice your craft—which the bonus scheme doesn't allow." (Plumber)

But among the general workers there was no greater tendency for the workers on Works A to refer to the importance of intrinsic rewards than workers in Works C even though it was the Works A men who did, in fact, describe their work as interesting.

In view of the emphasis placed upon the importance of security as a reason for coming to work at Seagrass, it was surprising to find that this was less

---

1 See Chapter 3, p.46.

often mentioned as a desirable aspect of a job, than, for example, good supervision, or good work mates. It might be argued that there will be a tendency to reply to general questions of the kind now being discussed by naming qualities which are felt to be lacking in what people have at the moment. Hence the emphasis upon good pay. But this would not then explain the almost equally heavy emphasis upon physical working conditions as important in making a job a good one, for the sample appeared to feel that their working conditions at Seagrass were good. [1] The absence of reference to security at this point in the interview must then remain a puzzle.

Other evidence for the preoccupation of tradesmen and general workers on all three Works with pay came from replies to two other questions. The first asked, without any prompting, what were the most important changes which could be carried out at Seagrass. A half of the tradesmen and 30 per cent of the general workers mentioned something to do with pay.

"More money obviously: if you've got more money you can do anything."

"The basic wage should be higher."

"Do away with the bonus."

"Better wages for shift workers."

The other important categories of reply referred to changes related to management and supervision suggested by 29 per cent of tradesmen and 15 per cent of general workers:

". . .less supervision. There are plenty of chiefs, but not enough indians."

"Better communication between top and bottom; better organisation; more efficiency."

and to better working conditions, mentioned by 15 per cent of tradesmen and 10 per cent of general workers.

This open-ended question was then followed by one which offered a list of possible changes (Table 5.6). It will be noted that the suggested improvements centred on changes of employment conditions, and did not refer to

---

1 See Chapter 3, p.35.

Table 5.6   "We have a list of things that could be done. . . Would you choose the one you would most like to see done?

Answers	Tradesmen	Works A	B	C	All General Workers
			Percentages		
Better Pay	49	62	56	32	44
Longer holidays	7	3	11	11	14
Shorter working week	9	8	3	10	6
Better promotion prospects	14	6	9	4	7
Improved shifts	5	10	–	12	6
Improved facilities for shift workers	5	3	–	6	3
Improved working conditions	5	1	1	5	3
Help with housing	–	3	9	6	5
Better redundancy agreement	–	3	1	4	5
Fewer regulations	1	1	7	4	3
Better sick pay scheme	3	–	–	–	1
Don't Know	1	–	4	6	3
Total:	100	100	100	100	100

any possible increases in job interest. But it is still significant that over 40 per cent of the sample chose better pay. When asked why they had chosen pay the vast majority replied that money was paramount. The Works differences here reflected once again the fact that the Works C men were more satisfied with their pay.

One indication of differing orientations to work might be provided by an investigation of the sample's attitude to 'getting on' and to promotion, particularly because it has been suggested that the 'traditional' views of the working class about collective solidarity are being replaced by individualistic instrumentalism. The first attitude would be represented by the worker who would refuse to become a foreman because this would represent "moving on to the other side". A fifth of the general workers said that they had taken the Seagrass job because it offered 'better prospects'. This phrase needs to be interpreted carefully, however, because 'prospects' seemed to be used as a general term, to include prospects of secure employment and rising pay as much as prospects for promotion. The Works C respondents assessed their promotion chances more optimistically than the Works A men, but there was no difference between them in their desire for promotion. Almost all of the general workers would have liked promotion, although it should be stressed that in their case 'promotion' would for the most part be to a higher job category. Even among the tradesmen, where promotion did mean a real change of status, to estimator (the man concerned with setting bonus rates), or to assistant foreman, the majority said they would like it if it was available, despite the low esteem in which the estimator was held because of his role in deciding on bonus. Neither tradesmen nor general workers were, however, very optimistic about their chances of promotion, only about 10 per cent rating it as good or very good. In so far as these data revealed any differences of expectation or orientations to work, it was between the tradesmen on the one hand, with their concern about the opportunities which the job provided for the exercise of their craft, and the general workers on the other. There was relatively little difference between general workers in the different Works.

Attitudes to Trade Unions

This remains true if we examine trade union activity. There is evidence to suggest that the level of participation in their trade union by the semi-skilled men at Seagrass was, in some respects, above average.[1] But the tradesmen at Seagrass were more involved with and committed to their union than the general workers. Seventy-three per cent of the tradesmen said they regularly voted in elections for shop stewards, as compared with only 52 per cent of the general workers. Only 23 per cent of the tradesmen said that they never attended union branch meetings compared with 37 per cent of the general workers (Table 5.7). At some time or another 26 per cent of the tradesmen had held an elected post in their union compared with only 15 per cent of general workers. A half of both tradesmen and general workers thought that their union did its job 'very well' or 'reasonably well' although among the tradesmen there was markedly greater enthusiasm for what was then the A.E.U. than for any of the other craft unions. (Table 5.8) The A.E.U.

1 See J. Goldthorpe et. al., 1968, op. cit., Chapter 5.

Table 5.7   "How often do you go to union branch meetings?"

	T.G.W.U.	A.E.U.	E.T.U.	All Tradesmen
Regularly	11	36	11	21
Occasionally	26	33	24	29
Rarely	23	23	32	27
Never	37	8	34	23
Don't know	3	–	–	–
Total:	100	100	100	100

Table 5.8   "How well do you think your union does its job?"

	T.G.W.U.	A.E.U.	E.T.U.	All Tradesmen
Very or reasonably well	53	69	48	52
Not very well or badly	40	29	48	43
Don't know	7	2	5	5
Total:	100	100	100	100

members also had a higher level of participation in branch meetings and in elections than the other unions.

There was, however, little variation between the general workers in the three Works either in level of union activity, or in what they thought of the union. There was no indication therefore, that the difference found between the Works in the frequency with which the 'cooperational' or 'conflict' view of industry was held, reflected any basically different orientation towards either individual achievement or worker solidarity if involvement with the union is to be seen as an indication of a collective approach. Indeed, it might be said that most Seagrass workers were pragmatic trade unionists. They judged their unions by what they got from them and the majority of the men, even the tradesmen, were in favour of fewer unions being represented on the site because this would both eliminate unnecessary inter-union rivalry, and would also increase bargaining strength (Table 5.9).

Table 5.9　　"Do you think the workers' interests would be better represented if there were fewer unions on the site? Why do you say that?"

Answers*	T.G.W.U.	A.E.U.	E.T.U.	All Tradesmen
Yes				
(i)　because one union would be more powerful	19	13	16	11
(ii)　it would cut out demarcation disputes	7	13	24	17
(iii)　it would reduce bickering	30	39	34	36
(iv)　we should have a chemical workers' union	5	10	8	7
TOTAL 'Yes'	61	61	63	62
No				
(i)　each trade must have its own union	25	24	24	23
(ii)　generally satisfied	8	2	3	3
TOTAL 'No'	27	31	29	29
It Depends	3	8	8	6
Don't know	9	–	–	3
	100	100	100	100

* More than one reason or no reason at all could be given for replying yes or no to the main question.

Because this study has been primarily concerned with the experience of work and its reaction upon management worker attitudes and relations, there may have been a tendency to understate the importance of trade union influence on the site. We have noted that management encouraged trade union membership among the general workers while not formally imposing a closed shop. Negotiations on pay and conditions were conducted at company level with national trade union representatives. The company, in the face of some opposition, was clinging to a policy of discussing such matters as fringe benefits with the Works Councils which had local and national counterparts. Representatives to the Works Council were elected from the Works and were in no sense trade union representatives.

But local interpretation of national agreements as well as local issues had to be negotiated at site level. No recognition was given to any shop stewards' committee, although the senior shop stewards were very powerful and would have liked such central recognition. We ourselves had direct experience of their power. We would not, nor could we, have carried out this study without their agreement and cooperation which was not lightly given. Subsequent relationships, however, were very close and helpful. The senior shop stewards did consult a great deal together and although there was some rivalry between the craftsmen and the general workers, there was a great deal of agreement and a common hostility to any intervention from the district level of their unions. The complexity of relations on the site could not be grasped unless it was recognised that the criticism of local management expressed by our sample was given a very active and militant expression through the medium of the activity of the site shop stewards.

Orientation of general workers and tradesmen

To return to the search for differences of orientation among the workers at Seagrass—one final piece of evidence confirmed that the significant differences lay not between the different groups of general workers, but between general workers as a whole and the tradesmen. This was in the area of comparisons with white collar workers on the site. Consistent with their sense of identity and status the tradesmen were more aware of differences in employment conditions between the manual and non-manual workers on the site than were the general workers. As Table 5.10 shows, only a fifth of the tradesmen said that no differences existed or that they did not know what they were. On Works A, however, 30 per cent of the general workers professed to be unaware or ignorant of such differences and on Works C very nearly one half. What the general workers were aware of particularly were the better fringe benefits, and in the case of Works A, the better money enjoyed by white collar employees. But 30 per cent of the tradesmen, in addition to

104

Table 5.10   Unprompted answers to the question "What do you think are the most important differences in conditions of employment between the staff and the payroll?"

Answers*	Tradesmen	Works A	B	C	All General Workers
		Percentages			
Better hours	26	9	13	4	9
More money	12	30	15	6	15
Better sick pay, pensions, holidays, etc.	23	35	35	22	25
Status differences i.e. 'snob value', 'class distinction'	30	9	11	18	13
Other answers	30	17	13	18	18
No differences seem to exist	7	11	13	16	12
Don't know	15	20	26	33	29

*   More than one answer could be given so the answers may total to more than 100 per cent.

these factors, also mentioned status consciousness, and the 'class distinctions' which existed on site.

Similarly, more of the tradesmen than general workers were in favour of giving what has been called 'staff status' to all employees on the Seagrass site and the 'egalitarian ethos' of the tradesmen was reflected in the reasons they offered. Forty per cent compared with only a quarter of the general workers, simply said that "everyone should be equal". Typical comments were:

> "Yes, why should we be any different to staff? Probably some of the jobs we are doing are more important than some of theirs."

and

> "We are all employed for one thing—the end product. If you are all working to one goal, you might as well be on an equal footing."

This last comment is particularly interesting in view of the large proportion of positive replies from the tradesmen to the 'teamwork' question.[1] It supports our argument that they saw the company as a team where their contribution was as essential and as important as any from technical or managerial levels.

Despite the fact that the tradesmen compared their own value favourably with that of white collar workers they also expressed a genuine egalitarianism which might well have existed somewhat uncomfortably side by side with their self-conception of their own importance. For it was the tradesmen who thought that significant groups of the general workers were underpaid. In reply to the question "Are there any groups of workers here who you think get paid too little for what they do?" a quarter said "tradesmen", but another quarter named process workers, 19 per cent tradesmen's mates, and 32 per cent the general labourers i.e. the lowest paid of the unskilled workers. General workers, however, answered this question almost exclusively as an extension of their own personal grievances about pay. They were also less likely to say that any groups were paid too much for what they did, whereas 70 per cent of the tradesmen thought that the white collar and supervisory grades were overpaid.

There is little in this examination of reasons for taking work at Seagrass, of general attitudes towards work, towards trade unionism or towards the stratification system in the work situation to lend any support to the view that the differences of attitude and behaviour between the general workers in the different Works could be linked to 'prior orientations' in a general sense. The one difference which has emerged is that Works C workers were younger on average, had a slightly different occupational background, and had heavier financial responsibilities. This might have led them to be more concerned about pay than men on the other Works. Yet the Works C men were, in fact, those who expressed most satisfaction with their pay, although they were also the most likely to take action to defend their pay levels. They were also the group most critical of their immediate work situation, and most likely to view that situation as management and men on 'opposite sides'.

Since our evidence pointed to the possibility that it was young married men with heavy financial responsibilities who responded to work constraints in a critical way, we should ideally have reanalyzed our material in such a way as to examine the individual attitudes of all people, no matter on which Works they were to be found, to see whether position in the life cycle rather than work situation might be the crucial variable which linked with differences of attitudes and behaviour. But unfortunately the data had not

---

1 See Chapter 3, p.45.

originally been analysed in a way which would have enabled this to be done within the time and resources available. As an approximation, however, we decided, despite the smallness of the sample, to divide the general workers within each of the three Works:

a) by age, between those under 30 and those 30 and over (Appendix Table 1).

b) by those paying a mortgage and those not (as a general indication of financial responsibility).

c) by those who had previously held either skilled (apprenticed) manual or white collar jobs and those who had only occupied semi or unskilled job (Appendix Table 2).

The attitude of these groups were then compared on the questions relating to job interest, satisfaction with supervision, "teamwork", reasons for coming to work at Seagrass and the three most important factors making a job a good one. The largest differences were between the age groups. Younger workers were more likely to have come to Seagrass because of the money and the security, and they were more likely to say that money was important in judging a job. They were more likely to hold an 'oppositional' view and to find their job boring (Appendix Table 1). When the sample was divided according to the kind of job held immediately before coming to Seagrass, it appeared that the people with higher status jobs were more likely to say that they had taken their present job because of the money. They were rather more likely to be satisfied with supervision, to find their job interesting, and they were far more likely to hold a teamwork view of management employee relations (Appendix Table 2).

But if we can draw any conclusions from these small samples, the Works influence was still extremely marked and consistent. Thus the young men on Works A were much more committed to a teamwork view and found their supervision more adequate than the young men on Works C. Similarly the men who had previously held white collar jobs or had been apprenticed and were now working on Works A were more likely to choose the teamwork analogy and to describe their supervision as adequate and their job interesting than were the people with the same background on Works C.

It seems highly plausible that younger men with family responsibilities will be more concerned with the monetary reward and security aspects of their work. But in this respect, they were merely demonstrating, in a heightened form, the general orientation of the whole sample.

To recapitulate the argument of this chapter, we have found that the general workers all placed heavy emphasis upon the extrinsic rewards of employment. They were looking for reasonable pay and good working conditions. When they took the job at Seagrass they were looking for security of employment by which they meant a low risk of being dismissed as well as the security provided by the pension and sick pay schemes. These wants and expectations could be seen to be very clearly determined by the social milieu in which these workers had grown up.

Works A men, however, happened to find themselves in a work situation which they found interesting and where they felt they could exercise judgement and initiative. They were paid less than the other Works and they were critical of their pay. But because they were, on average, older, the pay issue may not have been of such pressing importance for them. Works C men, on the other hand, found themselves in jobs which were relatively uninteresting and by the standards of the site, although not of their own past experience, in rather unpleasant working conditions. But they got high pay and they were the most satisfied of the groups with their pay. At the same time, they did have the heaviest financial responsibilities.

The Works A men, in terms of general satisfaction with supervision and of their actual behaviour appeared, at least temporarily, to have traded pay for job interest. But not so the Works C men, for their high pay did not wholly compensate for the boring job. Indeed, it might be argued that failing to find any 'intrinsic' work satisfaction, the maintenance of a satisfactory position on pay became doubly important, hence the number of walk-outs by the Works C men over issues concerned with bonus. This grievance activity would give these men some degree of control over their work situation as well as serving to maintain or to raise their earnings. For the present argument, however, the main point is that overwhelmingly, the Seagrass general workers shared an instrumental attitude to their work. In so far as there were differences of attitudes and behaviour between them they appeared to derive as much from what the worker himself *found* in the employment situation as from his prior expectations and orientations. On the other hand, the tradesmen were clearly very much influenced by their general occupational role and by the way their beliefs and expectations had been shaped in the process of acquiring their craft, that is by forces outside the immediate work situation at Seagrass.

5. Appendix Table 1 A Selected Comparison of Attitude of General Workers in Three Works by Age Groups

	Works A		Works B		Works C		All Three Works	
	Under 30	30+	Under 30	30+	Under 30	30+	Under 30	30+
Mentioning money as one of the three most important factors making a job a good one	77	52	47	49	77	48	65	50
Mentioning								
(a) Money	44	16	20	23	28	6	29	16
(b) Security	44	41	60	31	44	42	50	38
as reason for coming to Seagrass								
Firm is like a football team								
Teamwork	78	82	60	85	39	67	55	78
Opposite Sides	22	14	33	10	44	27	36	16
Other	—	2	7	5	17	6	10	5
Job Interest								
Interesting or about average	100	84	46	57	56	57	62	71
Boring	—	7	33	23	39	21	29	16
Other	—	9	20	10	6	21	9	13
Supervision—enough authority								
Yes	100	75	60	67	44	49	62	65
No	—	20	27	26	50	42	31	28
It varies	—	2	7	7	—	3	2	4
Don't know	—	3	7	—	6	6	5	3
Number of Cases	9	44	15	39	18	33	42	116

5. Appendix Table 2.

A Selected Comparison of Attitudes of General Workers in Three Works by Previous Occupation

	Works A		Works B		Works C		All Three Works	
	White Collar or Apprenticed	Other	White Collar or Apprenticed	Other	White Collar or Apprenticed	Other	White Collar or Apprenticed	Other
Mentioning money as one of the three most important factors making a job a good one	75	53	58	43	47	64	56	53
Mentioning								
(a) Money	25	20	26	20	24	9	25	16
(b) Security	25	46	47	35	53	38	44	40
as reason for coming to Seagrass								
Firm is like a Football Team								
Teamwork	100	76	74	80	76	47	81	68
Opposite Sides	–	20	21	14	12	44	13	25
Other	–	4	5	6	12	9	6	7
Job Interest								
Interesting or about average	91	85	63	60	70	50	73	67
Boring	8	5	26	26	12	35	17	21
Other	–	10	11	11	18	15	10	13
Supervision—enough authority								
Yes	92	76	68	63	53	44	69	62
No	8	20	21	29	41	47	23	31
It varies	–	2	11	6	–	3	6	4
Don't know	–	2	–	2	6	6	2	4
Number of Cases	12	41	19	35	17	34	48	110

6 The Environment of the Works

Works A, B and C each belonged to a different division of the main company. Overall company policy provided a common framework for the operation of the divisions in the ways described in Chapter 2. But as the study proceeded, the existence of certain important differences between the divisions became more apparent. Senior management often referred to the specific 'character' or 'atmosphere' of a particular division. Only a superficial acquaintance was needed to show that the relative importance of research and development, as compared with production or marketing problems, varied from division to division with the result that pressure was felt at different points in the total system of the division. Some of these differences could be traced to differences in the economic environment, others to the nature and extent of technical change. Yet others seemed to reflect management beliefs about the best way to run a works. In other words there seemed to be differences in the style of management. These factors could all have played a part in shaping what the worker found in his employment situation at Seagrass and might thus influence attitudes and behaviour.

The Economic Environment

It has sometimes been suggested that where labour costs form a small proportion of total costs there is less incentive to minimize total labour costs.[1] All three of the Seagrass works were capital intensive, but the capital output ratio was highest in Works A and lowest in Works C. As a result an 'easier' working atmosphere might have prevailed in Works A than in Works C. Works A management might have been more willing to make concessions which would make the work situation more attractive for their workers.

This hypothesis did not stand up well to further examination. Average earnings were higher in Works C than in Works A.[2] Moreover the overall labour policy of the company set very narrow limits on the discretion which individual works' management could exercise about pay. For instance any proposal to upgrade a job in Works A would be scrutinized very carefully at various levels in the company. Not only might it have serious implications for the rest of the Seagrass site, where the trade unions would be quick to use the

1 J. Woodward, 1965, op.cit., p.54—55.
2 See Chapter 3, p.55.

change for bargaining purposes, but it might also have repercussions in factories in other parts of the country which were more labour intensive.

Another aspect of the general economic environment which could have affected the amount of pressure experienced by first line supervisors and workers was the general state of the market for the divisions' products. A works enjoying a protected market might have felt able to afford a more relaxed policy. Moreover the impact of competition might be felt differently by the various departments of the divison. Strong competition which took the form of having to keep ahead with technical developments would have little effect upon current production and relationships with the general workers. The main impact would be upon the research and development department. In contrast, competition, which resulted in the search for immediate cost reduction, would be felt directly by the general workers through the imposition of ever more stringent quality standards, or pressure for a higher rate of output. In fact, however, the market situation of Works C was rather more protected at this time than that of Works A and B.

All three works manufactured technically advanced products, which had been developed by the company in the postwar period. All of the products were producer's goods but those of Works A were furthest back in the man-ufacturing chain. Most of the Works A output was further processed by its customers as raw materials, whereas Works B and C sold to customers who were in the consumer goods market. Being close to final demand the two latter works appeared more exposed to the immediate consequences of changes in consumer tastes or to other fluctuations in demand. In addition, more of their products were sold to non-company customers. Works A on the other hand sold two thirds of its output to other parts of the company, including Works C. This gave it an assured market. There were also some advantages in the fullness and reliability of the information available to it for the planning of production and in the speed of feedback of complaints about quality. Thus the first impression was that Works A was the most protected. But this was not the whole story.

Even within the company the Works A output was sold at world market prices and if, at any point, it could not meet its commitments to its company customers it had to 'buy in' additional supplies at market prices. Moreover at the time of this study both Works A and B were beginning to face consider-able international competition. In the type of production with which Works A was concerned total costs were fixed in all but the very long run, and operating below capacity soon eliminated any profit. International com-petition had led to some sudden sharp falls in world price in 1965 and to accusations by U.K. producers that foreign competitors were 'dumping'. The way to meet this competiton in the long run was seen to be through technical

112

advance to achieve ever greater economy of scale in the design of new plants. These developments were ultimately to have fundamental consequences for the general workers in Works A. But at the time of our study the immediate impact was small. There was little which production management could do with the existing plants to meet competition except to place ever greater emphasis upon the avoidance of breakdowns.

Works B was faced with similar competition for its products at about the same time, but because of differences in the technical process the consequences for the general workers were more immediate. A reduction in demand could be met first by a slowing down of the process which would be felt in the packaging and warehouse section as a reduction in workload. A larger cut back would result in the closing down of one of the production streams. Thus the men interviewed on Works B were far more aware of the difficult competitive situation facing their products than were the Works A men. In contrast with both of these works, however, Works C was in a favoured situation in 1965, for its main products were still protected by patent. The end of this period could be foreseen and this was reflected in the demands upon the research and development departments for the introduction of new varieties, but the general workers in production were not affected. The more critical attitudes found in Works C could not easily be explained, therefore, in terms of a less favourable market situation.

Technical Change

Innovation of process or product was a common response to the demands of the economic environment from all three Works. In Works C new varieties and improved quality were being worked upon. Some of the best operators were engaged in test production. But by 1965 there had been no major innovation which had any large scale repercussion upon working conditions or tasks in any part of the works.

Works A, too, was free from any technical change which might have an immediate effect upon the general workers. As the previous section indicated, the search for economies of scale had led to work beginning on the construction of a new, large, single stream plant with about four times the throughput of the old plants. Ultimately the new single stream plant was to result in considerable change in the jobs of the process operators particularly in its demands for greater care and alertness. But in 1965 the new developments appeared only to offer prospects of higher pay and expanding promotion opportunities in the future. Far from causing discontent among the Works A men, these visible signs of expansion appeared to contribute something to the feelings of greater contentment which they expressed.

113

HUNT LIBRARY
CARNEGIE-MELLON UNIVERSITY

The study showed, however, that technical improvements in Works B were not being incorporated in new plants so much as built into existing ones. One exception was a plant for a new product which, profit-wise, in 1965, was largely being carried by the rest of the works. Another was the beginning of mechanization in the warehouse section which was helping to make the jobs there more attractive. Elsewhere the changes on existing plants resulted in physical disruption of operating conditions which among other things helped to explain some of the greater criticism of working conditions in Works B than Works A. More important, however, was the fact that innovation was changing the tasks of the chemical process operators. For example, technical advance had reduced the amount of manual work which a man in charge of a reactor had to perform, but this enabled him to look after more reactors. Where before he had been tending one reactor, he ended up in charge of five. The intellectual element of his tasks had much increased, and he was required to supply greater attentiveness and speed of response. Some operators proved unable to meet the new requirements and were redeployed to easier tasks in other parts of the works. Such change naturally produced some dissatisfaction.

Superimposed upon these ongoing technical changes on Works B was a reorganization of first line supervision. The number of foremen was reduced, the responsibility of some assistant foremen and general workers was increased, and a few assistant foremen were moved to other jobs. This change was in no way a consequence of technical developments. Rather, it appears to have resulted from management's belief that it was desirable to enlarge the job of the operator and to give him more responsibility in order to increase job satisfaction. It was somewhat unfortunate that these well-meaning changes occurred at the same time as more responsibility was automatically being demanded of the operator by the technical changes described above. For he found himself called upon to adjust to increased responsibility and demands being made upon him from two directions.

It was not surprising, therefore, to find that the attitude survey showed less satisfaction among the men in Works B than Works A despite certain similarities of technology. Not only was there less satisfaction with job interest and with the quality of supervision, but the Works B men also displayed critical attitudes which seemed to spring directly from the experiences described in this section. They were more apprehensive about their security, and more reluctant to be moved to other work places in the plant.

Thus, it appeared that fears, which were the consequence of both the technical and administrative changes described above, tempered the general satisfaction of the chemical process operators on Works B. In Works A, technical change appeared to provide a general framework for the expansion

114

of opportunities which increased satisfaction. In Works C technical change was neutral. Explanations for the greater dissatisfaction of the men in this latter Works have therefore to be sought elsewhere.

Management Style

One tempting way to explain the observed differences of attitude and behaviour would be in personal terms, that is differences in the quality of senior management. There will always be "better" or "worse" managers who will personally contribute something to the state of morale in the organization which they control, but this study did not attempt to make any such assessment of quality. But some of the areas where the views of the workers seemed to diverge most markedly could well be situations where "style" was important.[1] The extent to which a firm was perceived as being like a football team is an example. Advocates and practitioners of a 'participatory' management style would presumably expect to find their employees agreeing that a firm is like a football team 'because good teamwork means success and is to everyone's advantage'. The views of such senior management might also affect the supervisor worker relationship favourably for there is some evidence that the attitudes and behaviour of first line supervision may themselves be correlated with the kinds of attitudes and behaviour exhibited towards them by higher levels of management.[2]

Management "style" however is difficult to define operationally. It is particularly hard to disentangle the influence of general sets of beliefs from the influence of the production system. For instance, the frequency and the quality of interaction between different levels of the hierarchy of management, and between management and operators, has sometimes been discussed as though it were an indicator of "style". It was said of Works A management, for instance, "that they always knew about any troubles brewing". Works A management also claimed that they consciously made efforts to keep in touch at all levels of the organization—i.e. that they had chosen to adopt a particular "style". But the differences between Works A and Works C in the frequency of such interaction, at least up to the level of plant or section manager, was in large part a direct consequence of the demands of the production system itself. If Works A management was in contact with

---

1 See Chapter 3, p.42.
2 E. A. Fleishman—"Leadership Climate, Human Relations Training and Supervisory Behaviour" in ed. E. A. Fleishman, *Studies in Personnel and Industrial Psychology*, The Dorsey Press Inc. Homewood Illinois, 1961. pp. 315–328. R. Dubin, G. C. Homans, F. C. Mann, D. C. Miller, *Leadership and Productivity*, Chandler Publishing Co., San Francisco, 1965, p.124.

workers in the course of the day to day running of the plant, it would certainly have every opportunity to appreciate the general worries and grievances of operatives. Even if close contact were the result of a conscious policy, however, this itself might not have been developed entirely independently of the demands of the production system. It might have been an example of the growth among management of:

> "different interpersonal orientations related to the nature of their task." [1]

Management beliefs may also influence the formal structure of an organization which, in turn, can influence the ease of communication and the degree of contact at different levels in the hierarchy. The formal organization chart of Works A was much simpler than that of either Works B or Works C. In Works A the hierarchy ran from assistant foreman to foreman, plant manager, section manager, assistant works manager to works manager. At the time of our field work there was an additional level in Works C. There was also a more complex functional organization to some extent in Works B, but especially in Works C. There was no time in the study to investigate the relationship between the formal and the informal management structure. This was an important omission. But it will be argued in the next chapter, that some of the greater complexity of formal organization in Works B and C reflected the greater complexity of the control mechanisms in those works, i.e., it stemmed from the demands of the production system. This would provide some objective basis for the complaints about lack of information and red tape on Works C. Nonetheless, it was interesting to note that after the field work for the attitude survey had been completed, there was a review of organization in Works C. As a result the formal structure was simplified. This seems to support Joan Woodward's finding that there may be more latitude in the choice of the appropriate organization structure in the large batch and mass production type of production systems, than at the extremes of the technical scale; that it is in this area of batch production that the technical and social ends of organization may conflict.[2] If the technology did allow choice the final structure adopted in Works C might have been determined by management beliefs about what was the 'best'. In the same way, the decision to reduce the number of supervisors in order to increase job responsibility in Works B, reflected a particular belief on the part of management about what made work tasks more or less interesting.[3] So although the technology set

---

1 Paul Lawrence and Jay Lorsch, *Organisation and Environment*, Harvard University Press, Boston, 1967, p.33.
2 J. Woodward, 1965, op. cit., p.145.
3 See this Chapter, p.114.

certain limits upon the structure of management in the different works, there was some room for differences of "style" to make themselves felt.

In areas other than formal organization, however, there appeared to be limits to the extent to which differences of "style" could emerge between the works. These limits were set by company policy itself. Strenuous efforts were made to ensure a uniform interpretation of labour policy by means of frequent joint works' managers' and personnel officers' meetings on the Seagrass site. At company level, although not frequent, interchange of personnel was not unknown at all levels of staff above assistant foreman, and there was certainly interchange of senior managerial personnel between the divisions. Thus, although divisions were thought of as having distinct characteristics which could rub off onto the works belonging to them, and to the managers working in them, there was also a company "style" common to all the divisions.

But this "style" could be said to have developed historically from the company's original interests in chemical production, where basic management problems were the maintenance of the smooth operation of complex processes, involving the use of relatively little labour. Output and quality depended as much upon the technical contribution of management as upon the attention or effort of operatives. Moreover since output and quality were often linked only indirectly to the effort of operatives, the bonus system was not a central instrument in management's armoury of control. Most of the process on Works C, however, was outside this central tradition of the company.[1] Yet its senior management was originally recruited from the chemical tradition. Some difficulties of adaptation were therefore to be anticipated and were brought to the fore most clearly just before this study began, at the point when there was an amalgamation of the textile interests of the Seagrass company with another company in the same field. The latter had developed in a mainly textile environment. Among other things this amalgamation revealed discrepancies in the nature and use of bonus systems in the two companies. The attitude survey was conducted at a time when the task of bringing the practices of the two organizations into line was in full swing. Some of the changes had repercussions on the operatives, and could have contributed to the greater degree of dissatisfaction found on Works C.

The size of unit

Another variable which should be discussed in this review of general environmental characteristics is the difference in the size of the Works. It is widely believed that the size of an industrial organization has a considerable

---

1 See Chapter 2, p.32.

influence upon workers' attitudes and behaviour and that generally the morale of the work force is higher in smaller than in larger organizations. Recently Ingham has published a thorough and critical review of the existing evidence which has been produced in support of this view.[1] His own interesting data, drawn from a comparison of attitudes in six small firms, employing less than 100 employees, and two large firms with over 3,000 employees, (with one exception all in the unit and small batch engineering production system) suggests that a process of self-selection may be at work:—

> "the workers who had selected the small, low-wage firms had done so in order to attain the high level of non-economic rewards provided by these organizations. From the workers' point of view the most important non-economic requirement was for complex and varied work tasks. A significant minority (about 20%) were attracted to the small firm in the first place by the friendly social—both peer and authority— relationships. On the other hand the workers who had selected the large high-wage plants were oriented to the attainment of high earnings: they were more narrowly economistic in their behaviour."[2]

The Works on the Seagrass site were not independent firms; nor, as we have seen, could any such major process of self-selection have occurred. Yet the pattern of attitudes and behaviour correlated with size in an anticipated direction. Works A, where attitudes were most favourable, was the smallest and Works C where they were the most unfavourable was the largest. But at this point it is worth asking what is the relevant unit whose size is to be considered. There were at least five levels, if not more, at which workers could view the organization. The first was at company level, encompassing all divisions wherever they were located geographically. The second was the site level of Seagrass itself. The third was the level of the Works with their separate managements responsible to different divisions of the main company. Fourth there was the plant or section within the Works and fifthly the immediate work group. The attitude survey suggested that the men themselves thought of the organisation as existing on at least two levels. Comments on payment and fringe benefits were couched largely in terms of the company nationally, whilst discussion of management and supervision were largely at Works or site level. The men in all Works were equally critical of the red-tape, regimentation and anonymity which they felt was a

---

1 G. Ingham—*Size of Industrial Organisation and Workers Behaviour*, Cambridge University Press, 1970.
2 Ibid. p.112.

characteristic of working at Seagrass. In this respect, apparently, it made little difference which Works a man was employed in; rather criticism related to the site and the general bureaucratic rules for social control of the labour force.

The men on the three Works also showed more or less the same level of criticism of management worker relations in general. But, as we saw in Chapter 3, there were some interesting differences between them in the actual frequency of contact with senior management, and in the suggestions which they made for improvements in their relations with management. Ingham has argued that workers in small firms value the personalised authority relationships which they find there. So that it could well be that the greater frequency of contact with senior management on Works A did contribute something to the more favourable attitudes found there, and that this was due in part to the relatively small size. Equally some of the criticism on Works C may have sprung from a feeling that management was particularly remote and that communication was difficult because the Works was so large. At the same time it is interesting to note that there were more accusations levelled at management that they were too status conscious on Works A than on Works C. In other words the Works A men saw themselves as part of a team and wanted more recognition of this fact, whereas on Works C the workers aspired mainly to improved channels of communication.

It could equally well be argued, however, that the presence or absence of team feelings sprang as much from the technology itself as from size. The demands of the production process required senior management participation in the day to day running of the plant on Works A far more than on Works C. In this case size was a function of the technology and not an independent variable. What may be equally important is the effective size of the work group, and this we shall discuss in the next chapter in so far as it affected first line supervision. But there was little evidence of strong attachment to peer relationships in the work group in any of the works. Most men working with others said that they would not mind if they were moved away from the particular men with whom they were working to other parts of the plant.

Summary

This review of general features of the environment of the three works should serve as a warning against drawing over simple conclusions about cause and effect relationships. Some aspects of the competitive situation, of the impact of technical change and of management "style" certainly appeared to be relevant to an understanding of the variations in satisfaction in the three works. The worsening competitive situation facing Works B had an adverse impact upon the general workers in a number of different ways. A sense of insecurity had developed among a group of workers who were generally known to set great store by security. Workers in Works B were also adversely affected by technical change which was imposing higher performance standards upon them. This additional stress was compounded by the conscious decision of management to give the general workers 'more responsibility'. It was perhaps not surprising, therefore, to find that the Works B workers felt their jobs to be less interesting, and their immediate supervision to be less satisfactory than the workers in Works A.

Works C was still in a relatively comfortable competitive position and the general workers were free from the impact of technical change. Their greater dissatisfaction probably did not stem from these sources therefore, but from the complexity of the formal management structure. This combined with certain aspects of the conflicts which management had to face arising from the need to reconcile chemical and textile management, could have contributed to some of the dissatisfaction on Works C. The extent to which such aspects of organization and management "style" were themselves influenced by or were independent of important differences in the production systems of the works was not, however, altogether clear.

Thus the complex of variables discussed in this chapter could be seen to contribute significantly to the shaping of the total work situation in which the general workers and supervisors were interacting. It remained for us to examine the way in which social relationships were themselves influenced and shaped by differences in the production system.

7 The control system and social relationships between supervisor and supervised

The character of the actual tasks which the general workers were engaged in and of the physical environment in which they had to work, differed so much between the Works that it seemed to go a long way towards explaining why men in Works A found their jobs interesting and men in Works C did not. What was less clear was why there should be any association between finding a job interesting and expressing favourable attitudes towards first line supervision. In the light of the work going on at Imperial College at this time, however, it seemed possible that the connection lay in the nature of the control system associated with the technology.

Control Systems

Within the term 'control system', Woodward and her colleagues encompass the total system for directing and controlling the production task, including the four elements of objective setting, planning, execution and monitoring. They suggest that:

> "The link revealed by the South East Essex studies between technical and organisational characteristics may in fact be a link between technology and the nature of the control system, on the one hand, and between the control system and organisational behaviour on the other." [1]

Just as the hardware of the production system, that is the type of machines to be operated, or material to be handled, puts constraints upon the worker which limit his possible range of behaviour, so too does the control system. Further analysis of the South East Essex material, together with new research, suggested that there were three characteristics of control systems which were significant for the understanding of organisational structure and behaviour. The first was the way in which control was exercised, whether it was through personal hierarchical authority, through impersonal and administrative procedures or through automatic mechanical control. It was suggested that it might be possible to position a firm on a scale ranging from

---

1 Tom Kynaston Reeves and Joan Woodward, "The Study of Managerial Control" *in* ed. J. Woodward, 1970, op. cit., p.39.

the use of personal hierarchical control at one extreme, to completely mechanical control at the other.[1] The second was the extent to which there was overlap or separation between, on the one hand, the design and programming system and, on the other, the execution system of the enterprise. The third was the extent to which there was unitary or fragmented control, the latter implying:

> "that there are a number of control criteria which people in an organisation are trying to satisfy at one and the same time. A particular task has to be completed by a predetermined date to satisfy the production controller: it may involve using certain methods to satisfy the work study man; and a limited number of people to satisfy the personnel manager; it has to comply with certain quality standards to satisfy the inspector; it should not involve more than certain costs to satisfy the cost accountant; and so on."[2]

Seagrass provided examples of both impersonal administrative and of automatic mechanical control. The sociological importance of this distinction is that, in the first case, the control procedures are impersonal in that the rules are laid down in advance, are applied impersonally and the outcomes measured or judged by specialist persons or departments at the periphery of the hierarchical authority structure of the organisation. Yet the channel of feedback is most likely to be via the normal authority structure, that is through the first line supervisor who will correct quality by instruction to the operator or who will have to justify the bonus payment if it is in dispute. With automatic mechanical control this personal feedback is increasingly eliminated. The system itself communicates directly to the operator whose task is then to take appropriate action.

In respect of normal social controls of employment all Works at Seagrass were alike. All supervisors had to ensure that their men were at their job within the specified working hours and obeying the normal working rules. But no detailed study was required to see that the Works A foreman did not have to deal with changes of variety of product whereas the Works C foreman did. Moreover, the design of plant capacity on Works A was the single most important determinant of the volume of output, whereas the effort expended by individual workers made some contribution in Works C. In the light of this kind of distinction we decided to investigate in detail how the bonus and quality control systems operated in the three Works, and what the consequences were for the social relationships between operators and supervisors.

---

1 Ibid., p.45.
2 Ibid., p.51.

The bonus system

Bonus systems can be regarded as impersonal administrative mechanisms of control over quantity and/or quality of production and are obviously most effective in manufacturing situations where the operator himself can influence these two variables. Of course, even in such situations they do not always have the desired effect, for operators may not respond in the expected way to the incentive offered. Moreover, other features of the administrative system, formal or informal, may work in the opposite direction and erode the expected effects of the bonus system.[1] But in many branches of the chemical industry the technical process itself and the design of the plant, rather than the operator, control the rate, and to a large extent, the quality of production. This was clearly the case in Works A, but not so obviously in the staple fibre and filament yarn areas of Works C.

The Company tried, however, to operate a uniform bonus system across all the Works. It had, therefore, to encompass such diverse activities as the individualistic inspection operations in Works C, where the pace and quality of work depended entirely on the operator, as well as the essentially teamwork process-controlled tasks in Works A. Shortly before the attitude survey a multi-factor bonus scheme had been introduced. It was based upon calculations of inputs of measured work together with allowances for other factors such as quality of output. Where appropriate, bonus was awarded on a group basis. By agreement with the trade unions concerned, the bonus ceiling was set at twenty-seven per cent of a man's basic earnings in his particular job category.

The consequences of the bonus system for the level of total earnings and for the weekly fluctuations in earnings varied considerably between the Works according to the nature of the technology. This can be illustrated by a detailed consideration of the experience of four different groups of workers; first, the chemical process workers on all three Works; second, the men in the warehouse of Works B; third the inspection groups in Works C and fourth, the machine operators in Works C.

In Works A the bonus team was a group of chemical process men (between two and four) working under an assistant foreman. These men could be operating either a plant, or a discrete part of a plant. Bonus levels could vary between teams, although such variations did not always appear justified to the men because the differences between the inputs of measured work were imperceptible to them. But the main point was that variations in weekly

---

1 See, for instance, Tom Kynaston Reeves, "The Control of Manufacture in a Garment Factory", *in* ed. J. Woodward, 1970, op. cit.

earnings were very small both between groups and within groups. Moreover in cases of breakdown a 'lieu bonus' was paid. Thus a common general source of criticism of bonus systems in process production—that the pay is lowest when the men are having to work hardest, as they do when a breakdown occurs—was avoided.

In the chemical plants of Works B variations in bonus payments between different groups of operators had been eliminated by treating all the plants as one bonus group; thus the same bonus was paid to all operators. For the same reasons as in Works A, bonus payments in the chemical area of Works B showed little variation from week to week. The chemical area of Works C had a system of bonus payments rather like that in Works A where men were organised in bonus teams operating different parts of the plant. But this was batch rather than a continuous chemical process and some effort was made to control the quantity of output by basing one part of the bonus calculations on the number of batches produced. However, the actual speed of production of batches depended more on the nature of the product and the process, and only marginally on the speed with which an operator could turn valves to empty tanks, and clean them out, so that the weight given to this factor was small and once again fluctuations in bonus earnings, although perhaps greater than in Works A, were also small.

In the warehouse and finishing section of Works B, each shift constituted a bonus team. The main criterion for bonus payments was the number of bags packed per shift. The operators in the warehouse could control the rate of production by their pace of working, and therefore had a high degree of control over their bonus rate, and it did sometimes rise above the twenty-seven per cent ceiling. The inspection area of Works C had a bonus system very similar to that of the warehouse and finishing section of Works B. Bonus was linked to output (that is the number of bobbins inspected) and the bonus group comprised the number of men working on a particular shift. The rate of production depended entirely on the individual operators, and as in the warehouse and finishing section of Works B, bonus earnings above the ceiling were not uncommon.

The biggest variations in bonus arose, however, in the staple fibre, and more especially, the filament yarn areas of Works C. In the staple fibre section the two main areas of production—spinning and processing—constituted two bonus teams. Movements, cleaning, amount of output and quality were taken into account when calculating bonus rates. Men would therefore lose bonus if the machines broke down, or if faults arose in the quality of the product. On the other hand, the constraints of the production system, that is the rate at which the machines were running, did not allow upward variation above the ceiling of twenty-seven per cent. In practice,

124

because of the large size of the bonus teams in this particular area, losses often tended to even themselves out. Nonetheless, there was more weekly variation in bonus than in any of the chemical process areas, and the variations sometimes appeared to be the result of factors quite outside the control of the operators.

In the filament yarn area, output and quality were again important components of bonus calculations. In the spinning area the bonus team was the shift team. Variations in the product presented the operators with different kinds of problems. Fine yarns were more likely to break, but heavy ones had to be doffed more frequently. Other variations also affected the bonus. It was the frequent changeovers of the machines from one type of product to another that had most effect. Production credits could be lost on the changeover shift, while men on the next shift could gain, despite the fact that they did not have to work as hard as the men who had changed the machines.

In the draw twist area a man's bonus group was determined both by the particular shift on which he was working and by the product he was making. The size of a bonus group varied between one man and twenty. The complex system of rotation from room to room already referred to, had been introduced in an attempt to give fair access both to 'better' machines and better bonus paying products. Despite this bonus earnings still varied considerably.

To summarise, it could be said that the bonus in Works A, and to a large extent in Works B, varied little because of the nature of the production system. Within the main areas of Works C it was sensitive not only to the efforts of the operator but also to the variety and type of product. Despite these differences in the way in which the bonus worked for them, the majority of the operators in all three Works voiced criticisms of the bonus scheme. The main complaint concerned the inadequacy of the method of calculation. In particular, it was argued that the bonus did not give enough weight to what the men considered to be the most important things, like the volume of production. But it was only in Works C that the bonus system became an issue around which grievance activity developed. Here was a situation where the men were performing a monotonous and restrictive task, and where they felt little sense of cohesion with the rest of the Works, but strong cohesion with the men on their particular shift. When these factors were combined with the difficulties of fluctuation in earnings, it was not surprising that the bonus was seized upon as an issue for dispute and as a basis from which considerable pressure could be exerted upon supervision and management.

Some of the characteristics and behaviour of the draw twist operators in Works C called to mind Sayles' 'erratic' work groups[1]. Their overall level of

1 L. Sayles, 1958, op. cit., p.18.

grievance activity was high, their participation in union activities was high and there was low evaluation of their performance by management. They did not share some other characteristics of Sayles' 'erratic' groups. They did not work as a team, nor were their jobs highly rated by other operators, except in terms of pay. But their tasks were extremely central to the total operations of Works C, they were homogeneous, there was a certain solidarity among the men on the same shift and there were few opportunities for promotion to other jobs. What is perhaps particularly interesting is that since the present research was undertaken, there has been a reorganisation in the Works which has reduced the sensitivity of the bonus system and there appears to have been a considerable change in the behaviour of these workers in that they are now much less militant. It must be pointed out that 'quick conversion to good relationships with management' is, according to Sayles, another characteristic of 'erratic' groups.

The quality control system

During the years immediately before the field work, Works A and Works B were both concerned with increasing the quality specifications of their products. This had an effect on the operators in both Works, in that they were working within continually narrowing limits. The nature of the quality control system, however, differed considerably between the two Works. In Works A it was mainly built into the production system. Dials showed the continuous analysis of the product and were read as an integral part of the operator's work. If they showed that the quality of the product was veering outside the prescribed limits, the operator concerned had to adjust his equipment to bring the quality back within the limits. Increasingly stringent quality specifications meant that the operator had to make adjustments more frequently as the area of 'slack' in the production system was systematically eliminated. The result of more detailed quality checks which were carried out by the laboratories were communicated directly to the operator. He acted on these results if necessary and, if he encountered any serious difficulties, called on his supervisor for help.

The situation in Works B was quite different. There was no built-in system of quality control on the continuous process plants of Works B. The results of regular quality tests by the laboratories were communicated to the supervisor and not to the operator as in Works A. This was necessary both because of the nature of the chemical process, and because of the variety of products made in these plants. It was the responsibility of the supervisor to remember and to understand the quality specifications of the many different products, and to take the necessary steps to correct the process by issuing instructions

126

personally to operators. Comparing the two Works one might say that Works A was a classic example of the operator's task becoming the 'control of control' and of control being almost completely mechanical. In Works B, differences in the chemical process, combined with the variation in products, made such mechanical control difficult. There was a well-developed impersonal administrative system of quality control but the supervisor played an important part in it. This had profound consequences for his role and his relationship with the operators.

The quality control system in the batch chemical area of Works C was very similar to that in Works B. The results of tests by the laboratories were communicated to the supervisor, who acted on the results, and if necessary instructed the operator to vary the process. But in the filament yarn and staple fibre area of Works C there were two ways in which quality could be controlled. The degree to which the process was operating smoothly in a technical sense was important in producing the required characteristics in the yarn and fibre. Quality was also affected by the way in which the operator did his job, for example doffing his bobbins at the right time, or avoiding putting greasy fingers on them. A sophisticated sampling system was used to produce charts of variations in aspects of quality. These charts indicated visually the limits within which it was acceptable to deviate from the standard. On the basis of information provided by this sampling method, it was the supervisor's responsibility to decide when and whether action was needed to rectify the quality of the products. He might also take action on the basis of direct communication from the quality control section. As has been indicated, the individual bobbins of yarn also went through a further stage of inspection, when they were visually examined and weighed.

A familiar situation in much of manufacturing industry is conflict between the need to produce the required quantity of goods but of the right quality and at the right time. In Works A this conflict did not arise at the point of production because control of quality and rate of production were built into the plant and the steps necessary to control quality were clearly defined by the technology. The position was similar in the chemical plants of Works B and Works C, and again there was little conflict between quality and quantity. Moreover, as we have seen the standards aimed at had little effect upon the earnings of individual operators.

In contrast, quality was given priority in the staple fibre and filament yarn areas of Works C and production had to stop or output be rejected if the standard was too low. The supervisor was called upon not only to respond to the quality control system by taking the necessary steps to rectify the process, but also to prevent faults by the individual operator, and see that the potential conflict between quantity and quality was resolved in a way

127

acceptable to the Company according to standards laid down. This reconciliation could affect bonus directly and meant that at least for the operator, the conflict between quantity and quality was a very real one which could be reflected in his pay packet.

It could be said that in Works A control over quality broadened the responsibility of the operator and encouraged a 'teamwork' relationship between supervisors and men because they worked together to solve the technical problems posed by the system. But in Works C outside the chemical process area, control over quality resulted in close supervision and increasing pressure on the operator from the supervisor. These differences, therefore, in the working of both the bonus system and the quality control system in Works A and Works C worked in the direction of increasing satisfaction in Works A but decreasing it in Works C. Moreover, the quality control system in Works C operated through the direct action of supervisors and this affected the social relationship between supervisors and men.

The Role of Supervision

In many firms the men known as assistant foremen on the Seagrass site would probably be called chargehands. A change of title and status in Seagrass had occurred a year or two before the attitude survey was undertaken. This regrading was in itself likely to have caused some stresses and strains, for the then existing chargehands did not necessarily possess the appropriate experience to fill their new role. But these men were certainly regarded by the operators as the first line of supervision.

The relationship between the operators and supervision varied in the three Works. In Works A the supervisor worked in a team with his men to maintain the flow of production. He was the person immediately called on when anything went wrong and close cooperation was needed during emergencies. In Works A the number of men supervised by an assistant foreman was never more than four, and was more often two or three. To revert to our earlier discussion about freedom of movement it was fairly easy for the Works A operator to take a break because a supervisor could keep track of this small number of men and the organisation of the work could be more informal. In fact, in Works A the assistant foreman was seen by management both as a 'leading operator' whose *work* was essential to maintain the process, and as a leader and controller of labour. However, for the purpose of our analysis, what is important is that the operators in Works A saw the assistant foreman as being in a position of authority. Even so, it was only in this Works that the foreman figured at all prominently as the person with whom operators would consult if they had problems with the

128

calculation of bonus, or complaints of any kind. In the other Works it was the assistant foreman who was usually approached. In Works A, therefore, contact between the operators and both the assistant foreman and foreman was close.

On Works A the typical pattern of interaction between worker and supervisor was one where the worker approached the foreman whenever he needed help. The supervisor had a trouble shooting role, where he was as likely to be required to offer advice as to give orders, although he would, on occasion, have to do that as well. Here is an example of the need to examine the nature of supervisory relationships in the context of the way in which the technology and the control systems associated with it shape the actual job which the supervisor has to do.[1]

Another related aspect of these various kinds of interaction between supervisor and operator is the influence it has upon the operators' perception of the source of the authority which the first line supervisor exercises. Following Talcott Parsons, Gouldner has identified two fundamentally different criteria for the legitimation of authority—authority based on technical knowledge and experience, and authority based on incumbency in office.[2] The men in Works A described the qualities of a good supervisor as first and foremost powers of organisation and leadership, followed very closely by good knowledge of the job. Over eighty per cent of them thought their immediate supervisor was able to deal with their questions and problems, and their satisfaction with their supervision stemmed from this recognition of technical superiority, leading them to say that their supervision was adequate and that in general the right men were chosen as supervisors.

In Works B, the supervisor was more of an administrator and organiser than a co-worker with his subordinates. He was the channel by which quality was controlled and frequent changes of production meant that much of his time was taken up with organising production changes and re-allocating men. To these characteristics of his supervisory role, which were determined in part by the chemical nature of the process itself and in part by the variety of products, must be added the fact, noted in a previous chapter, that a deliberate management decision had been taken to decrease the number of supervisors in the chemical process areas of Works B in order to enlarge the job of the operator. The assistant foreman in Works B, therefore, was much

---

1 R. Dubin, et. al., 1965, op. cit.
2 A. W. Gouldner, "Organisational Analysis" in ed. R. K. Merton, L. Broom and L. S. Cottrell, (eds.) *Sociology Today*, Vol. 2., Harper and Row, New York, 1965, p.413.

less available to give help. The fact that he was supervising more men also made it more difficult to allow freedom and flexibility in respect of informal breaks. There were more men for him to keep an eye on. He was still relied upon, however, to help in solving problems and in dealing with emergencies. The men in Works B looked for qualities of leadership and organization and they seemed, on the whole, to accept that their supervisor had enough authority to answer their questions and deal with their problems. But in Works B nearly twice as many men as in Works A thought that the wrong people were chosen as supervisors, and they were far more critical of the amount of discipline exercised over them. (It should be borne in mind in this connection, however, that strict enforcement of safety regulations was necessary.)

In the chemical area of Works C, the general role of the supervisor was very similar to that of the Works B chemical area supervisor, It was in the staple fibre and filament yarn areas of Works C that it differed to the greatest extent. In these areas a very large part of the supervisor's job was the organisation of production. He had to supervise and order changes in variety. Supervision would be called upon to help if technical difficulties did arise, but the work of individual operators had to be closely supervised and monitored in order to maintain full production and quality. A number of important changes in the supervisory structure in Works C have taken place since this study was made. But at the time we were on the site, the men, but not the assistant foremen, in the draw twist area were rotated between rooms, with the result that the supervisors were not able to build up a continuing relationship with the men working under them.

As we have already indicated it was here that bonus earnings were sensitive to the amount produced, so that the operators were likely to be very critical of any technical failure on the part of supervision to keep production running. Indeed, since no complex chemical reactions appeared to be involved, an experienced operator might well feel that he understood the mechanical limits of his repetitive tasks as well as his supervisor. The men in Works C thought the most important quality for supervisors was to know their job, and yet they were the most critical of their own supervisors' ability to deal with their problems. Thus the operators here looked to technical competence to legitimise the authority of the supervisor but felt that such legitimacy was often lacking.

One difference between the three Works which had been touched upon in this discussion of the role of first line supervision relates to the size of the work group controlled by one assistant foreman. In Works A the average number of operators working under one assistant foreman was about three. In the chemical areas of Works B and Works C, the work groups were larger, varying between eight and twelve men, while in the staple fibre and filament yarn areas of Works C one assistant foreman was responsible for up to fifteen men. In the warehouse of Works B and the inspection area of Works C about twenty men worked under one assistant foreman. Even where other elements in the task are the same, the larger the number of men a supervisor has working under him, the more difficult will be the social control of individuals and the greater the need to rely upon bureaucratic rules. In Works A, the size of the group controlled by an assistant foreman was small enough to allow for a high degree of personal flexible control and the granting of correspondingly greater discretion to the operator. In the warehouse and inspection areas of Works B and C some collective freedom could be granted because the process could be stopped and started at the discretion of the supervisor. But in the staple fibre and filament yarn areas of Works C, not only was the process continuous but the number of men under the control of one supervisor was such that he could not easily allow any flexibility.

The Tradesmen

This discussion has been concerned with the general workers, but it is interesting to consider the tradesmen's attitudes and behaviour against the background of this conceptual framework. We have seen that the tradesmen found their jobs interesting but that their consciousness of their craft skills made them critical of the amount of freedom they were given on the job.[1] They wanted a supervisor to know his job and to show his organising ability, but they were fairly critical of both the quality and authority of their actual supervisors.

The tradesmen were engaged on 'one off' jobs of repair and maintenance. Some of these would obviously be more routine than others, but the foreman's role was to programme the work. Upon his organisational ability, for instance, would depend how much of the tradesman's time was used productively. What the tradesman was to do, and to some extent how he was to do it, would have to be communicated personally through the foreman. Moreover even the bonus system would appear as a personal control system to the tradesmen. There was no simple measure of output, and because of the uniqueness of each job, estimators were employed to assess the time to be allowed for each job. Upon their assessments depended the tradesman's bonus. Hence the particularly vociferous criticism of the bonus system by tradesmen.[2] The control systems affecting the tradesmen were thus largely

See Chapter 3, p.53.
See Chapter 3, p.55.

experienced as 'personal' controls. In this situation it was highly likely that the legitimacy of the control being exercised over them would be challenged by the tradesmen, since it appeared largely to stem from incumbency in office rather than from any knowledge or expertise superior to that which they themselves possessed.

Conclusion

Some of the characteristics of the work task as discussed in Chapter 4 could probably best be thought of as consequences of the nature of the control system. For instance the amount of autonomy, of freedom to vary the pace of work and to move around, which the chemical process workers on Works A possessed, can be seen as mediated by the mechanical nature of the control system on that Works.

Moreover it appears that workers feel more favourable towards their supervisor when he is thought of as having technical expertise. How far the supervisor appears as a source of expertise is itself shaped by the production system. Expertise in, say, production scheduling is not so obviously a pre-condition of good performance, so far as the ordinary operator is concerned, as is expertise in dealing with a problem arising in a chemical process. So operators are likely to feel more favourably disposed to supervision which is demonstrably based upon superior technical skill which they can recognise as such.

It appears that the particular control systems in the different Works were very much influenced by the nature of the production process. In turn the kind of control systems influenced the nature and quality of social inter-action between operator and supervisor and were therefore of considerable sociological importance.

8 Conclusions

This study began by hypothesising that structures, attitudes and behaviour in the different Works at Seagrass were influenced by what we somewhat loosely called 'technology'. Thus technology, or the production process, was initially treated as an independent variable. In any complex situation where many variables are interacting it is helpful to be able to isolate one for comparative purposes and 'technology', in the Woodward sense, had the advantage of being definable and capable of being positioned upon a scale. The selection of technology was a methodological device. It did not imply any narrowly determinist position although, of course, it follows that we believed social behaviour to be influenced by the constraints placed upon it, in this case by technology in the work situation. We agree, therefore, with Perrow that:—

> "What is held to be an independent and dependent variable when one abstracts general variables from a highly interdependent and complex social system is less of an assertion about reality than a strategy of analysis. Thus no claim is made that for all purposes technology need be an independent variable." [1]

Much of the analysis has been concerned with expanding and refining the original definition of 'technology' and in identifying intervening variables between technology, attitudes and behaviour. This has led to the study of a wide range of factors from relatively simple things such as physical working conditions, to more complex and less easily definable concepts such as 'management style'. At the same time, we have recognised that any given collective human response to constraints is the product of the impact of those constraints upon the expectations, past experiences, in short orientations, with which people approach the situation in which they find themselves. It will also be influenced by constraints imposed from other directions, such as, in the Seagrass case, the trade unions to which the workers belonged. Hence, this analysis attempts an unravelling of some of the interplay making up the dynamics of the total social situation on the site.

Two methodological comments should be made at this point. Firstly, the treatment of the different variables in this case study might be regarded as

1 C. Perrow, "A Framework for the Comparative Analysis of Organisations". *American Sociological Review,* Vol. 32, No.2., April, 1967, p.195.

naive. We have made no attempt to apply any statistical techniques, choosing rather to be descriptive or to adopt an approach which has been called "opportunistic comparison". With a case study of this kind, we felt that a strategy which

> "focuses attention on a system of variables in interaction rather than on numerous variables considered additively"

would, at this stage, be more fruitful.[1] In one sense we were feeling our way towards the possibility of conceptualising some of the influences at work, rather than being in a position where we could quantify them or begin to postulate the nature of their inter-relationships. Secondly, it could be argued that what we have interpreted as congruence between the attitudes of a *sample* of men from different Works and the behaviour of all of the men in the Works was a matter of coincidence rather than of genuine association. Only a detailed correlation of behaviour and attitudes for individuals within Works would be conclusive. Nonetheless, contextual analysis is well enough established in the field of research into organisations to encourage us in the view that there was a meaningful link which called for explanation.[2]

Since this monograph was described as a contribution to an ongoing debate, the purpose of this chapter is to draw attention to those of our findings which may be important for future research. There are four such areas. First, we shall discuss how far and in what ways the concept of technology needs to be broadened to make it more meaningful and useful in the sociological study of organisations. Second, we shall discuss the extent to which this study has enlarged our understanding of the relationship between attitudes expressed by people about the work situation in which they are operating and their actual behaviour within it. Third, we shall discuss the implications of the often sharp contrasts in attitudes and behaviour between the skilled craftsmen and the semi-skilled, or general workers at Seagrass. Finally, in the light of our data, we shall attempt to evaluate the current discussion about the relationship between general orientation to work and workplace behaviour.

The Role of Technology
One of the major objects of the gradual expansion of the original study at Seagrass had been to explain more precisely the ways in which differences in

---

1 R. A. Peterson, "Must the Quest after Variance End in History?" in ed. M. N. Zald, *Power in Organisations*, Vanderbilt University Press, 1970.
2 J. S. Coleman, "Relational Analysis: the study of organisations with survey methods" reprinted—A. Etzioni, *A Sociological Reader in Complex Organisations*, Holt, Rinehart and Winston, New York, 1969.

the production technology of the Works could be seen to influence attitudes and behaviour of the operators employed in them. Using the Woodward classification of technology, we had found an association between technology and attitudes and behaviour which had been consistent with the findings of earlier research workers. In the continuous-flow production Works operators found their jobs interesting, and felt overwhelmingly that the amount of discretion they had in their work was adequate. These attitudes were associated with low levels of strike activity and absenteeism. Workers in machine-paced jobs on Works C, on the other hand, found their jobs boring, felt they had no freedom, and could not try out their own ideas. Their low level of satisfaction with the work they had to do was associated with a high level of absenteeism and a propensity to strike.

Early on in the study, however, we discovered that the individual Works at Seagrass were mixtures of technologies. Only Works A approached purity. Both Works B and C contained batch chemical process production alongside large and small batch production of dimensional commodities. Moreover, two Works which were using apparently the same dominant technology, when a relatively crude classification was used, were revealed on further investigation, to be different in a number of important respects. Works B was originally classified as a predominantly continuous flow process technology. But even in the chemical process area, it was markedly different from Works A. First, the chemistry of the process was different and did not lend itself to the kind of automatic control built into the Works A plants. Secondly, a number of different varieties of the product were handled in varying combinations depending upon customer demand. These two factors influenced the work tasks of the operators and supervisors and through this the kind of social interaction between them.

This finding is particularly interesting in view of the number of studies which appear to assume, for example, that all assembly lines are identical technology, and that since one assembly line is like any other, it will have the same consequences for the work of operators and supervisors. The speed of assembly lines varies and so too, does the variety of production, the quality standards and the procedures used for scheduling production. Such variations will certainly affect aspects of the operator's work task, while others will affect the job of the first line supervisor and the way in which his social role is structured. Which leads us to conclude, as we argue more fully below, that technology alone, even in the original Woodward sense, is not a sufficiently well defined independent variable for the comparative analysis of organisation.[1]

---

1 This is the view developed by Joan Woodward, herself and others in ed. J. Woodward, 1970, op. cit.

The Seagrass study confirmed, however, that one way in which technology, crudely defined in this way, did influence attitudes was through its effect upon the work environment, making it more or less pleasant, and also through its effect upon the content of the tasks which had to be done. There was a wide range of jobs at Seagrass, varying in the amount of autonomy and discretion they offered. Those which offered a great deal of autonomy were preferred by the Seagrass sample. In Works A, the operator was indeed, as we have described him, a "controller of control". He could vary both the sequence and pace of his work and he could also develop a rhythm of his own, take breaks and move about the plant pretty freely. In the materials handling and inspection jobs in Works B and C, the operators did not have much autonomy or discretion to vary the sequence of tasks, but they could vary their pace of working and, within limits, their stopping and starting times. Their level of bonus payments was also responsive to their efforts, sometimes individual, sometimes collective.

It was in the staple fibre and filament yarn areas of Works C that the operators lacked autonomy and discretion in almost all respects. They were allocated to a particular machine and most of their effort was controlled by the pace of the machine. Bonus could not easily be manipulated, although it could fall below the general ceiling through no fault of the operator. It could vary with a changeover in variety or because of a breakdown. The meaning of the concepts of autonomy and discretion as aspects of the task require further exploration so that a finer and less subjective classification of work tasks may be arrived at. As Perrow points out, the presence or absence of the opportunity to exercise discretion is a different thing from non-routineness.

"...discretion involves judgements about whether close supervision is required on one task or another, about changing programs and about the interdependence of one's task with other tasks." [1]

The Works A chemical process workers' tasks were routine when all was going well. Yet they were the men who had most opportunity to vary the task sequence and pace of work and they had to exercise discretion when things were not going well. The problem as Perrow himself recognises is one of operationalising these kinds of distinction.

These differences in the nature of the work tasks were reflected in a startling variation in the proportion of men on the different Works who said they found their work interesting—from only 26 per cent on Works C to 72 per cent on Works A. Yet the jobs of all of these men would be described as

---

1 C. Perrow, 1967, op. cit., p.198. Works A men probably exercised discretion in this sense when there was a crisis.

semi-skilled manual in traditional classification systems, and would represent a relatively narrow spectrum of jobs when set in the context of the distribution of occupations in the total economy. We have no means of knowing by what standard the men were making these judgements about the interest of the work. There was certainly no evidence that many of them had come to Seagrass in search of the means of satisfying desires for intrinsically interesting work. This indicates how badly more research is needed to establish how an interesting job becomes part of a manual worker's expectations, or at all central to his requirements from work.

A number of other studies support our conclusion that in the case of the tradesmen this expectation is central, and is established during the period of apprenticeship.[1] Ingham is one of the few people who has explored this question to a limited extent for semi-skilled workers. He has done this in his attempt to account for the much greater priority given to non-economic rewards by workers in small plants. He argues:

> "Variations in the value attached to non-economic aspects of industrial work are likely to be the result of prior work experience of different kinds of jobs during which time the workers' priorities concerning non-economic rewards are developed. . . Therefore expectations with respect to non-economic rewards are likely to develop gradually and to vary with type of industrial experience." [2]

The only evidence Ingham can produce shows that a significant group among the semi-skilled workers in his large plants had spent most of their lives in white-collar work, and it is this group who are least likely to define industrial work as a source of non-economic reward, presumably because they have been led to expect industrial work to be routine and boring.

> "Only those workers who *expect* to receive or are at least aware of non-economic rewards in industrial work are likely to be dissatisfied in their absence." [3]

It would be interesting to know, however, how the experiences of those semi-skilled workers who had always been in manual jobs had shaped their expectations. As we argue above, the evidence from Seagrass would seem to suggest that the general workers had not entered employment there in search

---

1 J. Goldthorpe, et. al., 1968, op. cit., p.25 and G. Ingham, 1970, op. cit., p.138.
2 G. Ingham, 1970, op. cit., p.137.
3 Ibid., p.138.

of, or expecting to find, interesting work. When they found it they viewed it rather as a windfall, a piece of good luck. This experience appeared to influence some of their behaviour in the work situation, but would it influence their behaviour if they had to leave Seagrass? Would they then look for interest in their work, and if they did not find it be dissatisfied? These are some questions for future research, although our judgement at the moment is that for the great majority of semi-skilled workers necessity dictates and has always dictated a preoccupation with the 'extrinsic' aspects of work—pay, security and working conditions—when the employment relationship in its totality is considered.

The next problem which emerged at Seagrass was why interest in the job should be so closely related to favourable attitudes to supervison. Positive attitudes were most in evidence in situations where supervision appeared closest in a conventional sense because the ratio of supervisors to supervised was there highest.[1] The differences in attitude to supervision between people doing similar types of job, but on different Works, was one of the things which had directed our attention to the possible significance of the supervisors' role.

It became clear that while some aspects of this role were dictated by the technology, (the hardware of the plant and the recipes in use), others were dictated by the various systems devised for controlling aspects of the production task. Thus the foreman and assistant foreman's job in the chemical process area of Works B involved him in close personal supervision of the operators, partly because of the volatile nature of the chemical process, undoubtedly an aspect of technology. But the need to switch production from one variety to another also meant that he had personally to direct the activities of the operators and to move them from production train to production train. In the drawtwist area of Works C, the supervisor was personally responsible for the feed-back of information about quality to the operator. He also had to direct activities to obtain the required volume of production and to direct the changeover of variety. So the control system, in the sense discussed by Woodward and Kynaston Reeves, emerged as an important independent or intervening variable.[2] Works A had a unified and mechanical control system which was almost completely built into the hardware. Works B and C had a fragmented and impersonal administrative control system for parameters such as quality, quantity and cost. But significantly, the feedback to the operator from this impersonal system was mediated

---

1 See the discussion of span of control in P. Blau and W. R. Scott, *Formal Organisations; a Comparative Approach,* Routledge and Kegan Paul, London 1963, p.168—169.
2 T. Kynaston Reeves and J. Woodward *in* ed. J. Woodward, 1970, op.cit.

personally through the verbal instructions of the supervisor. Parallel with this spectrum of control systems it was possible to identify a spectrum of supervisory roles, ranging from that of cooperative "trouble shooter" where the supervisor assisted because of his superior technical knowledge, to what might be described as a 'policing' role, exercised by the supervisor because he occupied the role of supervisor.

From the viewpoint of the operator and supervisor, therefore, the important constraints in the work situation stem both from the production process itself and from the control systems associated with it. The reason for referring above to the control system as either an *independent* or an *intervening* variable is that, in some situations, the type of control system is clearly and narrowly dictated by the type of technology, whereas in others it is less obviously so. For instance, computerised control, with mechanical feedback to the operator, is only possible when the relevant production variables can be identified and the inter-relationships between them specified. In such situations the control system may be embodied in, and become part of the hardware. In other situations, the constraints imposed upon the design of the control system are less narrowly determined by the technology itself.

Some control systems are primarily shaped by characteristics of the market. Varieties of the commodity will be produced in response to market demand and the assessment of the nature of this demand and the 'need' for variety may be more or less objectively determined. The Company can have precise information about specific customer requirements. On the other hand management may have a view of the market which is more influenced by subjective perception than objective requirements.[1] In either case, however, the parameters of quality, cost, etc. are less likely to be well known, or narrowly defined, and a far more complex system of administrative control is likely to emerge.

This case study supports the view that the introduction of control systems as an organisational variable represents an advance upon any simple classification of technology. When certain characteristics of the control system are known it is possible to describe their consequences for social relationships between first line supervision and operators. But other questions remain. The nature of the control systems adopted appears to be a function of the complexity of the production system, which in turn, is related to uncertainty

---

1 For a discussion of the possibility of choice existing for management, and the consequences of choice upon control systems and behaviour within the firm, see T. Kynaston Reeves and Barry A. Turner, *A Theory of Organisation and Behaviour in Batch Production Factories*, 1970, unpublished paper, Imperial College, London.

or variety. But uncertainty has different sources.[1] Works B illustrates this very well. There we encountered uncertainty in the chemical process itself i.e. in the technology as well as uncertainty arising in the market from the need to meet varying customer needs. Can these different kinds of uncertainty be quantified; can a distinction be made between objective and perceived uncertainty; and can the consequences of uncertainty for organisational structure and behaviour be more closely specified? These are some of the questions which seem to us to be of great importance for further research in this area.

The relationship between attitudes to the work organisation and workplace behaviour

The fact that attitudes to the work task varied between the Works but did not vary towards management in general, underlines the fact that workers may hold differing and not necessarily consistent attitudes towards different aspects of the organisation by which they are employed. All workers at Seagrass, craftsmen and semi-skilled alike, were agreed about the good aspects of employment there. They valued the security and what they considered to be good physical working conditions. They were agreed, also, in their criticism of management and management worker relations. Those attitudes of the general workers which appeared most significantly associated with differences in "constraint evasive" behaviour at Works level—that is, higher absenteeism and labour turnover, greater incidence of unofficial stoppages, and greater pressure on management—were a low level of interest, indeed a high level of frustration, in the job itself, and criticism of first line supervision. This criticism was not of personal relations with the assistant foreman or foreman, but rather of his competence and ability to do his job. The majority of the general workers in all three Works said that they got on well with their assistant foreman. Such replies might be expected when an individual is asked to describe his personal relations with another individual. There will be strong normative pressure to avoid criticism of *a* particular person. At Seagrass, critical attitudes to supervision, which varied between the three Works, emerged only when the men were asked to assess various aspects of the individual in his role as supervisor.

---

1 See also Perrow's discussion of "the number of exceptional cases encountered in the work" or the predictability of the raw material, and "the nature of the search process that is undertaken by the individual when exceptions occur", which may be well understood or not well understood. C. Perrow, 1967, op. cit.

But the experience of the general workers employed in Works A, B and C at Seagrass must be placed in a more general context. The fact that the degree of control over their particular work situation varied between the Works, did not mean that there was any variation in the extent to which the men felt they could exercise control over more general and universal aspects of their employment situation. Their different experience of supervisory relationships in particular Works may, at times, have appeared relatively unimportant compared with their general experience of the basic employment relationship. They were all semi-skilled Seagrass workers subject to the usual kind of social controls. They had to accept the works rules, work shifts and clock on. They were all affected by the nature of the wage effort bargain and by other issues of job regulation.

If we concentrate for a moment, not upon the differences, but upon the similarities of attitudes and behaviour exhibited by the Seagrass semi-skilled workers, then it appears that even though they thought of the Company as a good employer, were generally disposed to describe the relationship between management and workers in teamwork terms, and in the main expressed a desire to remain in the employment of the company, they were nonetheless a militant group. Certainly the management of the Company regarded Seagrass as a 'difficult' site at this time, and the general workers were believed to be more ready to act against management policies than general workers employed elsewhere in the same Company. And if Seagrass semi-skilled workers in 1965 were compared with, for example, the Luton affluent workers in 1962, then their record was certainly more militant.[1] But, as we argued in Chapter 3, most employees expressed overall positive feelings towards their employer. Nonetheless, this did not prevent them from putting as much pressure as they could upon management. The only attitudes expressed by the sample, which seemed to relate to this generally higher level of constraint evasive behaviour on the whole site, were the criticisms of management worker relations, of management competence and of the anonymity of employment on the site.

But here the general values of the social milieu from which the Seagrass men were drawn cannot be ignored. It was a homogeneous 'traditional' working class area where the tradition of collective trade union action had strong roots. Nor should the presence of militant craftsmen on the site be discounted. The craftsmen regarded the general workers as "Carnation Milk" creatures, as one shop steward put it. By this he meant that, by his standards, they were docile and easily persuaded by management. As we have suggested, the general workers were certainly not immune from the influence of the

---

1 See J. Goldthorpe et. al., 1968, op. cit., p.72 footnote 1.

tradesmen.[1] One of the craft shop stewards at this time had a charisma which extended far beyond his own union, and which certainly had an impact upon the behaviour of the general workers' own leaders'.

Thus there is no simple association to be postulated between expressed attitudes and behaviour. The Seagrass workers would see nothing inconsistent in expressing favourable attitudes to some aspects of their employment position whilst in a particular situation, going on strike, or imposing an overtime ban. The general norms of the community, the nature of the influence and leadership offered by the trades union, as well as the constraints of the immediate work situation, all contributed in the final event to a very complex interplay of forces.

The Tradesmen

The importance of the influence of the tradesmen upon the general workers suggests the need for a fuller discussion of the significance of the attitudes of tradesmen themselves. Superficially, their behaviour was very similar to that of the Works C general workers—a high level of grievance activity, coupled with high labour turnover and absenteeism rates. But there was a strong suggestion in our material that the basis of the tradesmen's militancy was different from that of the Works C men.

On some issues the tradesmen held views very like those of the general workers. They valued the welfare schemes and amenities offered by the company and they also criticised what they saw as bad management and the 'anonymity' of employment at Seagrass. Like the general workers, the most important things they looked for in a job were money and good working conditions.

In other respects, however, the attitudes of the tradesmen and general workers diverged sharply. The tradesmen did not value highly the security of employment offered by the Company. But this did not mean that they did not feel secure. The difference lay in the fact that their confidence was founded on the belief that their own skills *earned* them security, not that they were dependent upon a particular employer. Consequently, they were less committed to the Company and expressed a willingness to move if 'something better turned up' and many were looking or had looked for other jobs.[2] They were less likely than the general workers to find their jobs boring. Indeed, they *expected* interesting work and were frustrated when they did not find it. They were more sensitive than the general workers to gradations

1 See Chapter 5, p.104.
2 For similar behaviour from craftsmen in the Luton sample see J. Goldthorpe et.al., 1969, p.59, footnote 2.

of status within the Company, and many felt that their own work contribution was undervalued. This constellation of attitudes can be termed 'craft consciousness'. It was this craft consciousness which supplied the tradesmen with a sense of self-worth which was significantly lacking among the general workers and which led them to take a broader view of many problems than the general workers. They had more decided attitudes on most questions and they were also aware, at least, of the problems of lower paid semi-skilled workers. But their first concern was with their own position. The very frustration expressed by the tradesmen when they felt their ability to do 'a good job' was being interfered with, and the readiness with which they took action to protect 'their' craft, indicates the importance which they attached to their own sense of identity.

The tradesmen working on the Seagrass site were not unique in this respect. Evidence of this 'craft consciousness' may be readily found in other studies:—

> "The craftsmen, on the other hand, while gaining some direct reward from the nature of their work-tasks, appear frequently to experience frustration in other non-economic aspects of their jobs; notably in regard to their desire for autonomy and responsibility and for the conditions they believe essential for 'good workmanship'. And this frustration would seem to be at the root of their critical attitude and often uncertain commitment to their employers . .the craftsmen, one could say, are most obviously the group with important wants and expectations relative to work which are left inadequately fulfilled." [1]

Or, to quote from a study, of the shipbuilding industry, located in the North East like Seagrass:—

> "The craft group then can be seen both as a moral community and an interest group. The members of a craft group have a sense of exclusive competence in the use of certain tools and techniques and a belief in their right to protect this area against the encroachments of other groups." [2]

It is this 'craft consciousness', we would suggest, which formed the basis for the 'militant' behaviour of the tradesmen on the Seagrass site. It

---

1   J. Goldthorpe et. al., 1968, op. cit., p.37.
2   R. Brown and P. Brannen "Shipbuilding". *Sociology*, Vol. 4, No.2., May, 1970, p.200.

is not the same as a 'class' consciousness which reflects a view of inherent conflict in society between employer and employed. Indeed, the craftsmen were rather more likely than the general workers as a whole to see the industrial organisation as a 'team'. Their efforts, however disruptive to teamwork they may have appeared at times, could then be seen as directed towards ensuring that their own place in that 'team' was adequately recognised. They were certainly concerned to stress verbally the identity of 'shared interests'.[1]

Although the behaviour of the Works C men was as militant as that of the tradesmen, its source, we would argue, was of a radically different kind. Not that the Works C men's militancy sprang from a conflict view of society any more than did that of the tradesmen. Rather, their rejection of the football team analogy appeared to reflect their experience of the *immediate,* rather than the general, work situation. They found themselves in 'conflict' with management over a wide range of immediate issues. In many respects, the Works C men closely resembled the 'affluent workers' of the Luton study.

> "His work is not voluntary but imposed, *forced labour*. It is not the satisfaction of a need, but only a *means* for satisfying other needs." [2]

But unlike the Luton "affluent" workers, the Works C men did not seem to have made any trade-off of boring work for high pay; or if they had, they certainly seemed to find it an unsatisfactory one. It is worth noting, however, that some of the affluent workers of Luton (the assembly line men, closest in terms of work constraints to the Works C men) engaged in violent industrial action shortly after the fieldwork there had ended, while, on the other hand, apparent industrial 'peace' reigned in Works C in the year following our fieldwork, when new bonus rates had been settled upon. This suggests that a characteristic of this type of constrained work situation is its instability. The reaction of the workers concerned will be unpredictable. The uneasy relationship between effort and reward of both the Works C and the Luton workers has been well described by Westergaard.

> "For if the prototypical worker is tied to his work only by the size, security, and potential growth of his wage packet—if his commitment to the job and to everyday cooperation with the foremen and managers depends essentially on the fulfilment of such monetary conditions—his commitment is clearly a brittle one. He may be willing to accept the

---

1 See above Chapter 3, p.45–46.
2 Karl Marx, "Alienated Labour" quoted in Goldthorpe et.al., 1969, p.180.

lack of other interests and satisfactions in the job, for the sake of the money. But should the amount and dependability of the money be threatened, his resigned toleration of the lack of discretion, control and "meaning" attached to the job could no longer be guaranteed. The "cash nexus" may snap just because it is *only* a cash nexus because it is single-stranded; and if it does snap, there is nothing else to bind the worker to acceptance of his situation." [1]

If this is the case, extrapolation from attitudes to behaviour will be particularly hazardous because the policy and influence exerted by the workers' own leaders, or by management itself may well be the major factor determining which kind of behaviour predominates at a particular point in time. Moreover, the question must be asked whether at Seagrass the Works C workers were the only group bound to their employment by the 'cash nexus'?

Orientations to Work

These considerations lead naturally into the debate about the importance of general orientations to work in any explanation of attitudes and behaviour. Here we shall consider more closely the arguments put forward by Goldthorpe, Lockwood and their colleagues, particularly in "The Affluent Worker: Industrial Attitudes and Behaviour". The position adopted by these writers has already been outlined in the first chapter of this volume. Briefly, they argue that explanations of industrial behaviour must first be sought in the orientations which men bring to their work: —

> "The manner thus in which they define their work situation can be regarded as *mediating* between features of the work situation objectively considered and the nature of the workers' response." [2]

and then also:

> "For example, as we have seen, where men are orientated towards their employment in an essentially instrumental way, situations which from the point of view of 'human relations' theory would appear potentially pathological do not necessarily prove to be so." [3]

---

1 J. H. Westergaard—"The Rediscovery of the Cash Nexus" in ed. R. Miliband and J. Saville, *The Socialist Register, 1970*, Merlin Press, London, 1970, p.120.
2 Goldthorpe et. al., 1968, op. cit., p.182.
3 Ibid., p.179.

Thus a particular orientation to work will play a large part in determining attitudes to, and behaviour in, the job a man is doing. Moreover, where there is a choice of employment, a process of self-selection may occur, where workers with particular wants, stemming from their orientations to work, will tend to converge in industries which satisfy these wants. Thus a particular work situation may be characterised by a certain constellation of attitudes shared by the workers within it.

Three 'ideal types' of orientation to work have been identified as (a) instrumental, (b) bureaucratic, and (c) solidaristic.[1] These could be described as being exhibited by three types of worker (a) 'new' affluent workers (of which the Luton sample was held to be an example), (b) 'white collar' workers and (c) 'traditional' manual workers. It was argued that the 'new' affluent worker, with his instrumental orientation towards work, was proto-typical. These were the kind of attitudes and values which the manual worker of the future would increasingly display.

The most important finding to emerge from the Seagrass case study, how-ever, was that despite the difference in background between our sample and the Luton workers, the Seagrass workers appeared no less instrumental in their approach to their employment. The differences of composition of the two samples were considerable. First, only a tiny minority of the Seagrass men had ever lived anywhere outside the area, whereas 70 per cent of the Luton respondents had lived outside the Luton area up to the time of their first employment.[2] Secondly, the locality in which the Seagrass site was situated was a homogenous working-class area. Only a narrow range of alter-native employment opportunities were available; the area had experienced very serious unemployment in the inter-war years, while even in the post-war period unemployment rates had been above average. Luton, on the other hand, had been selected as an area for study precisely because of its 'newness, instability and openness', and for its "economic expansion, 'optimism' and relative isolation from older industrial regions".[3]

The Luton sample had been limited to include only married men between the ages of 21 and 46, regularly earning £17 a week gross in October 1962, (that was then above average male earnings in manufacturing industry). This was a deliberate research strategy to select a case which would be as favour-able as possible for the confirmation or rejection of the thesis of embourgeoisement of the working class, with which the research team was concerned. The Seagrass sample, on the other hand, was randomly selected,

---

1   Ibid., p.38., ff.
2   Ibid., p.150.
3   Goldthorpe et. al., 1969, op. cit., pp.43–45.

and 30 per cent were over 46, 10 per cent were unmarried and nearly half were earning less than the then national average wage.

The questions we put to our sample were not precisely the same as those used in the Luton study and we could not, for instance, compute any score of 'instrumentalism'.[1] But all the emphasis placed by the Seagrass men, in judging jobs in general, in the reasons for coming to work on the site as well as the reasons for staying in their present jobs, was 'extrinsic' in character. The four main considerations were the level of pay, the security of the job, the good welfare benefits and good working conditions. Intrinsic satisfactions deriving from the nature of the job itself were hardly mentioned by the semi-skilled workers, either as being a necessary feature of a hypothetical 'good job', nor as a particularly rewarding feature of their present jobs. In fact, 'job interest' was offered as a reason for staying in their present employment by far fewer of the men at Seagrass than of the Luton sample.[2] Nor did the Seagrass workers give any evidence of being more attached in any solidaristic sense to their workmates than the Luton sample.[3]

On these sort of measures, therefore, the Seagrass men appear to be at least as 'instrumental' as the Luton respondents. We would include even the tradesmen in this primarily 'instrumental' characterisation. Although it is true that they laid considerably more emphasis than did the general workers on the importance of intrinsic features of the job, 'instrumental' criteria came a very clear first when assessing jobs in general.

There was one interesting difference however. For the Luton workers, the main attraction of their present jobs was the level of pay. In the case of the Seagrass sample, the emphasis on money emerged not in relation to their present jobs but as the most important feature of a good job 'in general'. Unlike the Luton workers, the aspect of their present employment most valued by the Seagrass men was 'security'. By 'security' they meant security of employment i.e. that they would not be unemployed. There were also suggestions that security meant the regularity of income which was guaranteed, at least minimally, by the sick pay and pension systems. There

---

1 Goldthorpe et.al., 1968, p.160.
2 The questions were not identical. Seagrass men were asked "What are some of the things you like best about working for . . .?" Ten per cent of the tradesmen, 20 per cent of Works A, 2 per cent of Works B, 6 per cent of Works C general workers said that it was an interesting job. (See Chapter 3, p.35).
3 Twenty-two per cent of the Seagrass sample who were working in a group expressed concern about being moved away from their mates while in the Luton sample, 27 per cent said they would have been fairly or very upset. (Goldthorpe et.al., 1968, op.cit., p.51).

was no indication of what was claimed for the Luton workers, that security was interpreted

> "more in relation to long-run income maximisation than to the minimum requirement of having a job of some kind".[1]

The reason the Seagrass workers laid so much emphasis upon security is obvious in the light of the employment history of the area. Although we have no details of the employment experiences of the men we interviewed, they must have been aware of the generally unstable situation. Many of them had worked previously in the steel and shipbuilding industries which neither in the past, nor the present, offered very regular employment. Several small steelworks had closed down shortly before our fieldwork began and some of the men we interviewed had then been made redundant. In contrast, the Luton workers had little experience of unemployment.[2] In this situation we would argue that the Seagrass workers' emphasis on 'security' was as 'instrumental' as the emphasis of the Luton workers on monetary rewards. The Luton sample was, of course, younger, and we had found that there was perhaps a greater tendency for the younger workers at Seagrass to emphasise the level of pay as an important aspect of a good job in general and as a reason for coming to Seagrass in particular. But they also showed a slightly greater tendency than older workers to mention security as a reason for taking work on the site. It seems unlikely therefore that the difference in the age composition of the samples at Luton and Seagrass accounted for the different priorities which were expressed.

But if both Luton and Seagrass workers looked for extrinsic rewards from work, there was also little doubt that the attitudes of both groups were shaped by general social experience. Thus we would agree with Goldthorpe and his colleagues that:

> "little systematic association was revealed . . .between their immediate experience of their work situations as technologically conditioned, and the range of attitudes and behaviour which they *more generally* displayed as industrial employees".[3]

---

1 Ibid., p.29. In any case we find it difficult to find support in the data as presented for the Luton sample for this interpretation and if 'security' does have the same meaning for the Luton as for the Seagrass workers then the attitudes of the two samples come even closer together.
2 Ibid., p.117.
3 Ibid., p.181 (our emphases).

'More generally displayed' would relate to the attitudes of the Seagrass workers as employees of the Company. Yet, as we have demonstrated within this general framework, different attitudes and behaviour *within the work situation* could be manifested by different groups of workers largely in response to the differences in the prevailing technologies and control systems.

The discussion of the Luton data inevitably raises the question of whether, at Seagrass, we were encountering general attitudes which were increasingly belonging to a past era. Were the Luton workers really prototypical? If we want to make predictions about 'new' industrial workers, a particularly interesting group to study on the Seagrass site were the general workers of Works A. Their jobs represented the paradigm of automation, more so than any of the industrial groups in Luton. We have shown that they manifested very favourable attitudes to the job itself. They found it interesting, and they felt they had opportunities to try out ideas which they valued. They also got on very well with their immediate supervision. Was this an expression of what Blauner had found among his chemical workers, namely:—

> "a high degree of consensus between workers and management and an integrated industrial community in which employees experience a sense of belonging and membership".[1]

Was there evidence on Works A of any increased identification between management and workers? It was true that absenteeism, labour turnover, and the level of industrial disputes were lower on Works A than elsewhere, but we also found little evidence of positive identification with the firm. The men there were as critical of management, and the 'anonymity' of the site, as the other groups of workers, and they were as instrumental in their general orientations to work. They were more critical of their level of pay than Works C, although unlike Works C, they had not, at least at the time of our fieldwork, put much pressure on management to change this.

In the case of Works C, we would argue that the constraints imposed by the technology were *predisposing* factors making for discontent which expressed itself around the bonus and pay levels. Had pay levels not been as high as they were on Works C the discontent might have been greater. On Works A there was a wider divergence between expectations and realisations in respect of pay but satisfaction with supervision and the interest of the job appeared in part to compensate for this. This is not to say, however, that the behaviour of the Works A men reflected any 'integration' with the employing organisation. Indeed, all the evidence seemed to suggest that if pay levels on

---

1   R. Blauner, 1964, op. cit., p.178.

Works A got too far out of line with the men's expectation of what was reasonable in regard to pay elsewhere or in relation to their view of their responsibilities, 'militant' behaviour might well follow. Evidence in support of the view that the Works A men retained a calculative involvement with the Company was provided by later events on the site when a productivity agreement was introduced and ran into a great deal of opposition. Works A men were not noticeably more cooperative than those on the other Works. Our data also showed that they were as involved as other workers with their trades union. Moreover the first strike to affect process workers at Seagrass occurred recently.

Even if the Works A men showed few signs of being integrated in a positive or 'moral' way with the Company, it was possible that the value to them of the intrinsic interest of their work might ultimately result in the development among them of attitudes at least similar to those held by the tradesmen. As we noted earlier, more of the Works A men were likely to say that there should be a chemical workers union, which might be taken to indicate that they were beginning to consider themselves a 'craft' group.[1]

But there are two important barriers to the development of a 'craft consciousness' among chemical process workers. The first is that they cannot enjoy the sense of independence from any *particular* employer which a tradesman possesses. The skills of the Works A men cannot be bargained with in an open market: they are dependent upon the prospects of one particular industry. The second barrier, linked to the first, is that the skills they possess were not acquired as part of a unique socialising process, which characterises the apprenticeship of the craftsman. The most that seems likely to develop in the longer run is a sense of industrial identity such as that which characterises the workers in the steel industry. But here we feel we have returned to an area where more work needs to be done in relation to the development of standards of expectations about work.

---

1   See Chapter 5, p. 103

Summary

One major limitation of the Seagrass study is that it stopped at the factory gate. We cannot even begin to suggest what impact the work experience of the men we studied had on their lives outside of work, upon their family and social life, their aspirations for the future, or their political attitudes. And we can only indicate one or two directions in which their experience in the community reacted upon their attitudes and behaviour at work.

This case study has, however, provided a further understanding of the dynamics of the situation where there is interplay between the influences operating outside and within the workplace. At one level of analysis what was happening at Seagrass must be understood in terms of a group of workers with primarily instrumental attitudes to work, committed for the most part to collective action through their trade union representation, not apparently holding any clear ideological position about the power structure in the industrial situation or in the total society, but directly experiencing conflicts of interest between themselves and their employers which had to be bargained about. The significant variation in this general position was that of the tradesmen, who were far more independent in their attitude to management than the general workers. At another level of analysis, that is within the specific work setting, other differences of attitude and behaviour emerged in response to the specific constraints imposed by the technology and the control system. These made themselves felt through two channels, the structuring of the job itself on the one hand, and, on the other, through the way in which supervisor and operator relationships were shaped. Thus it would seem that an approach to the study of behaviour in organisations which uses a comparative approach may still fruitfully take as *its starting point* technology and the systems which management devise for the planning and execution of the task. We would expect such an approach to shed light on certain aspects of behaviour related to the immediate organisational situation. For explanations of industrial behaviour at a more general societal level other starting points are required.

Appendix—The Interview Schedule

1. First of all, could you tell me how old you are?
    . . . . .years

2. How long have you been with the Company?
    Under 6 months
    Over 6 months—1 year
    Over 1 year—18 months
    Over 18 months—2 years
    Over 2 years—3 years
    Over 3 years—5 years
    Over 5 years—10 years
    Over 10 years

    If broken service, record
        (i)   Year of first employment
        (ii)   Last date of joining

3. (a)   What is your job now?

    (b)   What grade/category is that?
    Tradesmen-grade. . . . .
    or general workers-category. . . . .

    (c)   Is that shift or day work?

4. (a)   What job were you doing before you came here?
                  First job . . . . : . . . .
    Occupation . . . .
    Industry . . . .

    (b)   How long were you in that job?
    . . . . years
    . . . . months

    (c)   Why did you leave it?

5. What other jobs have you done in the last ten years and how long were you in them?

6. How did you hear about this job? **Record verbatim then code**
   Through the Labour Exchange
   Newspaper or other advertisements
   Came or wrote on spec.
   Heard through friends or relatives
   Other
   DK, or can't remember

7. Why did you decide to join the Company in the first place?
   Record verbatim, then code all that apply
   Good/better money
   It was a job
   Good prospects
   Security
   Because friends or relatives worked there
   Interest/job/trade
   Good firm to work for
   Location
   Other
   D.K., Can't remember

ASK OF GENERAL WORKERS AND MATES ONLY

. (a) Were you in the labour pool when you first came here?
   Never in pool
   Still in pool
   . . . . weeks/months
   If ever in pool
   (b) What do you feel about the system of putting a man into a labour
   pool before giving him a job in the works?

ASK ALL

. What are some of the things you like best about working for the
   Company?

0. What are some of the things you like least about working for the
   Company?

   Now I'd like to ask you about the pay and hours
1. What were your gross weekly earnings last week including bonus and
   overtime, **before** tax or any other deductions?

153

12. (a) For the sort of work you do here, would you say your take-home pay is:
Very reasonable
Reasonable
Unreasonable
D.K.
(b) Why do you say your take-home pay is reasonable/unreasonable?

13. Do you know of any firms around here which would pay you more?
Yes
No
IF YES
(i) Which firm(s) is that?
(ii) What type of work?

14. Looking at the other jobs in this firm, either hourly, weekly or monthly paid, would you say there are any where the men get paid too much for what they do?
Yes
No
It depends
D.K.
IF YES
(i) What jobs are they?

15. Looking at the other jobs in this firm, either hourly, weekly or monthly paid, would you say there are any where the men get paid too little for what they do?
Yes
No
It depends
D.K.
IF YES
(i) What jobs are they?

16. Do you think that the rate of pay for different kinds of jobs in the works should vary according to the abilities of the man doing the job?
Yes
No
It depends
D.K.
Why do you say that? (What else should be taken into account)

17. Do you think there are any other things which should be taken into account when deciding on rates of pay?
   - Yes
   - No
   - It depends
   - D.K.

18. What differences to your life does working overtime make?
   If money, probe: What about other things?
   Record verbatim, then code all that apply
   - Money
   - Less family life
   - Less social life
   - Other
   - D.K.

FOR SHIFT WORKERS ONLY

19. As a shift worker are you satisfied with the extra rate which you receive over a day worker?
   - Yes
   - No
   - D.K.

   IF NO
   What would you consider a reasonable difference per hour?
   . . . . p

20. (a) What are the main disadvantages of shift work from the point of view of your family and social life?
   RECORD VERBATIM
   (b) What are the advantages?
   RECORD VERBATIM

ASK ALL

21. If you had the choice of, on the one hand, working 3 hours less a week and getting the same money as you do now, or on the other hand, working the same hours as you do now, and getting more money, which would you choose?
   - the same money but 3 hours less
   - the same hours with more money
   - D.K.

   INTERVIEWERS (if asked)
   More money = 3 hours at overtime rates
   Now about the bonus scheme . . . .

155

22. Generally speaking, would you say the system on which your bonus is calculated is fair or not?

        It is fair
        It is not fair
        D.K.

23. Have you heard of a system they have here called a good work bonus?

        Yes
        No

IF NO   Give examples

24. Do you think more use should be made of such special payments for special efforts?

        Yes
        No
        D.K.

RECORD COMMENTS

25. At the moment your wages go up and down each week according to how much bonus or overtime you get. In some companies the wages are averaged out so that you get the same amount each week. (This means that you would not get as much as you get in your best week, but more than in your worst week. But over the year you would get about the same amount of wages.) Would you prefer this system?

        Yes, averaged earnings
        No, fluctuating earnings
        D.K.

Why do you say that?

IF NO

Would it make any difference if you were guaranteed that wage?

        Yes
        No
        D.K.

RECORD COMMENTS

26. As you know, staff have a salary which doesn't fluctuate from week to week, and they may have to work overtime. Sometimes they get paid for this, or they may take time off in lieu. If your wages were averaged out, and guaranteed, would you be prepared to do this?

RECORD VERBATIM, THEN CODE

        Time in lieu
        Overtime pay
        Both
        Neither
        D.K.

Why do you say that?

27. As you know, the Company has a profit-sharing scheme which means that anyone who has been with the Company for a year may get an annual bonus in the form of Company stock. What do you feel about this scheme?
RECORD VERBATIM
What do you think the Company had in mind when it introduced this scheme?
RECORD VERBATIM
Do you think it has been successful in doing this?
RECORD COMMENTS

28. Do you think that the present sick pay arrangements from the workers point of view are
      Very reasonable
      Reasonable
      Unreasonable
RECORD COMMENTS. PROMPT IF NECESSARY Do you think people ever take advantage of it?

29. (a) When you were thinking of coming to work here did you know whether they had a pension scheme?
      Yes
      No
      D.K.
IF YES
(b) Did the pension scheme influence your decision to come here at all?
      Yes
      No
      D.K.
RECORD COMMENTS

30. (a) If you had the choice now, would you stay in the pension scheme
   OR leave the pension scheme?
(b) And if you had the choice, would you stay in the State Graduated Pension Scheme
   OR leave the State Graduated Pension Scheme

31. (a) What do you think of the Company pension scheme. Do you think it is
      Very reasonable
      Reasonable
      Not very reasonable
      Unreasonable
      D.K.
(b) Why do you say that?

32. (a) Let's take an imaginary example: Suppose for some reason you had to leave this job, and you had a choice between two other jobs, (the same as each other and your present job in all other respects). Which would you choose?

A job with

        (a) A pound a week less than your average wage with a sick pay and a pension scheme

OR (b) Your present wage without either a sick pay or a pension scheme

        D.K.

If (b)

(b) But if it were 50p a week less which would you choose?

    (a)

    (b)

    D.K.

(c) Why did you make that choice?

33. (a) If the choice were between a job with:

        (a) A pound a week more than you get here without sick pay or pension scheme

OR (b) The same wage as you get now with sick pay and pension schemes (i.e. exactly the same as now)

        D.K.

Which would you choose?

IF (a)

(b) But if the choice were 50p a week more, which would you choose

    (a)

    (b)

    D.K.

IF CHOICE AT QU. 32, 33 is different (i.e. either aa or bb)

(c) Why do you say that?

34. What do you think are the most important differences in conditions of employment between the staff and the payroll?

RECORD VERBATIM

If clocking in is mentioned, prompt—anything else?

If clocking in is not mentioned

Some people do not have to clock in when they arrive, but you do. What do you feel about this?

35. (a) In some firms they have given all workers staff status. Would you favour such a change here?

    Yes

    No

    D.K.

(b) Why do you say that?

36. What do you think are the three most important factors in making a job a good one?

37. Are there any other payroll jobs in this plant which you would rather do than your own?
        Yes
        No
        D.K.
IF YES
 (i)   Which job is that?
(ii)   Why would you rather do that job than your own?

38. Is there anywhere else on the site you would prefer to work? (Not in this plant).
        Yes
        No
        D.K.
IF YES
 (i)   Where is that?
(ii)   Why would you prefer to work there?

What about working conditions
39. (a)   What do you think of the working conditions in your own plant?
Prompt if necessary, things like lighting, heating, toilet facilities, noise, fumes and so on.
        Good
        All right
        Bad
        They vary
        D.K.
   (b)   Are there any improvements you would like to see in these conditions?
        Yes
        No
IF YES   What?

40. What do you think of the safety arrangements in your works?
        Adequate
        All right
        Inadequate

41. Do you think that the management takes a real interest in safety or do they only pay lip service to the safety arrangements?
        Interest
        Lip service

It depends
Other
D.K.
RECORD COMMENTS

42. The accident rate is now higher than it was 2 or 3 years ago. Why do you think this is so?
RECORD VERBATIM

43. (a) How about the canteen facilities? Would you say they were:
Good
All right
Poor
It varies
Premises good, food bad
D.K.
(b) Do you use the canteens or not?
IF NO, Why not?

44. Do you belong to any social or sports clubs here?
Yes
No

45. Would you like to see any more or different facilities for out-of-work activities?
Yes
No
IF YES Have you anything special in mind?

46. (a) How do you get to work?
Car
Bicycle
Motor bicycle
Public transport
On foot
More than one way
(b) How long does it take you?
Under 5 minutes
Over 5 up to 15
Over 15 up to 30
Over 30 up to 60
Over 1 hour
(c) How much does it cost you?
.... p. per week

47. (a) Do you think the Company could do anything to help with travelling?
    Yes
    No
    IF YES
    (b) What do you think could be done?

48. Now I'd like to ask you something about the job itself. Generally speaking, do you find your job is:
    Interesting
    About average
    Boring
    It varies
    D.K.
    RECORD COMMENTS

49. Does the job give you a chance to try out ideas of your own?
    Yes/sometimes
    Rarely
    Never
    D.K.
    RECORD COMMENTS

50. Do you have enough freedom on the job? Do you think
    Too much is left to you
    You don't have enough say
    It's about right
    D.K.
    RECORD COMMENTS

51. (a) Do you work by yourself or with others?
    Works alone
    With Others
    IF WITH OTHERS
    (b) How would you feel if you were moved to another part of the works, doing the same job as you are now? (That is working with different people.)
    ASK ALL

52. Do you yourself prefer to work by yourself, or with others?
    Alone
    With others
    D.K.

53. (a) Would you say the people in this firm were
       Very friendly
       Friendly
       About average
       Unfriendly
       Very unfriendly
       D.K.
    (b) Why do you say that?

54. What do you think about the rules for employees? Would you say there are:
       Too many
       Not enough
       About right
       D.K.

55. (a) Do you think discipline here is strict or easy, or about right?
       Too strict
       Easy
       About right
       D.K.
    (b) Why do you say that?

56. (a) How secure do you think your own job is?
       Very secure
       Secure
       Insecure
       D.K.
    (b) Why do you say that?

57. (a) If for any reason the management wished to terminate your employment, how much notice do you think they ought to give you?
       . . . . .weeks
    (b) Why do you say that?

58. (a) And if for any reason you wished to leave your job here, how much notice would you feel you ought to give the management?
       . . . . .weeks
    If he refers to agreed 4 weeks
    (b) Do you feel that is long enough?
       Yes
       No
       It depends
       D.K.
    (c) Why do you say that?

162

59. Taking everything we've talked about into account, that is, pay, hours, working conditions, fringe benefits, and the job itself, would you say you were:

        Very satisfied
        Satisfied
        Dissatisfied
        Very dissatisfied
        D.K.

RECORD ANY COMMENTS

What about training for the job . . . .

60. Did you serve an apprenticeship? If so, in what trade?

        No apprenticeship
        Still serving apprenticeship
        Started but gave up
        Completed here
        Completed elsewhere

For those who have not served apprenticeship here

61. (a) What training, if any, have you had since you came here?
    (RECORD TYPE AND LENGTH OF TRAINING)
        None
        Training now

    (b) Do you think the training (you have received) is
        Very adequate
        Adequate
        Inadequate
        D.K.

    (c) Would you have liked any more or different training? (Would you like)
        Yes
        No
        D.K.

IF YES

    (d) What would you have found/find helpful?

Now I'd like to ask you a few questions about supervision and management generally.

62. (a) Who is your immediate superior? **(Title of job, not name)**
    (b) Do you think he has enough authority to answer your questions and deal with your problems?
        Yes
        No
        D.K.

RECORD ANY COMMENTS

63. Is the supervision you get from . . . . (immediate superior)
        Very adequate
        Adequate
        Not very adequate
        D.K.

64. Would you say you get on with your. . . . .(immediate superior)
        Very well
        Reasonably well
        Not too well
        Poorly

65. What qualities do you think are most important for . . . .
(immediate superior)

66. On the basis of these qualities, do you think that, generally speaking they choose the right men here as (immediate superior)
        Yes
        Sometimes only
        No
        D.K.

67. Do you think you have the qualities to make a good (immediate superior)?
        Yes
        No
        D.K.
And what about the foremen?

68. Do you find getting help from your foreman, when necessary?
        Easy
        About average/not too bad
        Not very easy
        Difficult

69. Would you say you get on with your foreman
        Very well
        Reasonably well
        Not too well
        Poorly

70. If you were fairly sure there was a mistake in your bonus one week, who would you see about it?
> Recognised channels
> Chargehand
> Assistant foreman
> Foreman
> Estimator
> Shift clerk
> Shop steward
> Other (specify)

71. If there was quite a lot of overtime in your department and you thought you were not getting as much as other people in the department, who do you think you would go to about it?
> Recognised channels
> Chargehand
> Assistant foreman
> Foreman
> Estimator
> Shift clerk
> Shop steward
> Other (specify)

72. If you had any other complaint about anything to do with your work or your working conditions, what would you do about it?
> Recognised channels
> Chargehand
> Assistant foreman
> Foreman
> Estimator
> Shift clerk
> Shop steward
> Other (specify)

73. (a) If an hourly-paid worker of ability wants promotion, how far up the firm do you think he could rise?
RECORD VERBATIM, THEN CODE
> Assistant foreman
> Foreman
> The top (specify)
> Other (specify)

(Interviewers—if 'the top'—ask "What do you mean by that?")
(b) Do you think you could do this?

74. What would be the next job above yours now that you would expect to get if you got promoted?
        Leading hand
        Chargehand
        Assistant foreman
        Foreman
        Estimator
        Other (specify)

75. (a) Would you like to be promoted to this job?
        Yes
        No
        D.K.

    IF NO
    (b) Why is that?
    IF YES
    (c) Would you say your chances of getting this promotion are?
        Very poor
        Poor
        About average
        Good
        Very good
        D.K.
    (d) Why do you say that?

76. Would you say that chances of promotion in general here are
        Much better than most
        Better than most
        The same as most
        Worse than most
        Much worse than most
        D.K.

77. (a) Do you think the relationship between management and workers could be improved or not?
        Yes
        No
        D.K.

    IF YES
    (b) In what ways?

78. (a) Do you ever come into contact with senior management in the course of your work? (That is people above the foreman)
        Yes
        No
        D.K.

IF YES
(b)   Who are you thinking of there? (Title, not name)

79.   (a)   Do you think you see enough of senior management in the works?
              Yes
              No
              D.K.
       (b)   Why do you say that?

80.   Do you think you are told enough in advance
       (a)   About things likely to affect your work?
              Yes
              No
       (b)   About things happening in the plant generally?
              Yes
              No

81.   (a)   Do you think the Works Council serves a useful purpose?
              Yes
              No
              D.K.
       (b)   Why do you think that?

82.   (a)   Have you put any ideas to the management through the
              suggestion scheme?
              Yes
              No
       IF YES
       (b)   What happened?

83.   Now to go on to something else:
       (a)   Are you a member of a trade union?
              Yes
              No
       IF NO
       (b)   Why is that?
       IF YES
       (c)   Which union do you belong to?
              T.G.W.U.
              A.E.U.
              E.T.U.
              Other (specify)
       (d)   When did you become a union member?

84. (a) Have you ever held an official union post, or been a shop
        representative?
        Yes
        No
    IF YES
    (b) What post did you hold and when?

85. How often do you go to union branch meetings? Would you say you
    went—
        Regularly
        Occasionally
        Rarely
        Never
        D.K.

86. How about voting in the elections for shop stewards? Would you say you
    voted—
        Regularly
        Occasionally
        Rarely
        Never
        D.K.

87. How well do you think your union does its job? Do you think it puts the
    views of the employee to the management
        Very well
        Reasonably well
        Not very well
        Badly
        D.K.
    RECORD COMMENTS

88. (a) Do you think the workers' interests would be better represented
        if there were fewer unions on the site?
        Yes
        No
        It depends
        D.K.
    (b) Why do you say that?

89. Here are two opposing views about industry generally—I'd like you to
    tell me which you agree with more.
    Some people say that a firm is like a football side, because good
    teamwork means success and is to everyone's advantage.
    Others say that team work in industry is impossible—because employers

and men are really on opposite sides.
Which view do you agree with more?

Team work
Opposite sides
It depends
Other
D.K.

90. (a) Would you like to stay here?
Yes, until I retire
Yes, so far as I can see
It depends
No
D.K.

(b) Why is that?

IF YES

(c) Have you ever thought of leaving?
(i) Have you ever done anything to get another job?
If so, what did you do?
Hasn't tried
Looked around (no applications)
Applied unsuccessfully
Offered job, didn't like it
Other (specify)
(ii) Why did you stay in the end?

IF NO

(d) Have you done anything to get another job? If so, what did you do?
Hasn't tried
Looked around (no applications)
Applied unsuccessfully
Offered job, didn't like it
Other (specify)

91. Why do you think people leave here?
RECORD VERBATIM

92. What would you say to someone who was thinking of coming to work here, if he came to you for advice?
RECORD VERBATIM

93. We have talked now about quite a number of things which you like and dislike about work here. What do you think are the most important changes that could be carried out?
RECORD VERBATIM (If they mention wages, probe for other things)

169

94. Finally, can I ask you a few questions about yourself?
     Where are you living now
     How long have you lived there?
                Less than 1 year
                Over 1—3 years
                Over 3—7 years
                Over 7—10 years
                Over 10 years (not always)
                Always

IF NOT ALWAYS
95. (a)   Where did you live before?
     (b)   Why did you move?

96. What age did you leave school? . . . years

97. Are you
                Married
                Single
                Widowed/separated/divorced

IF EVER MARRIED
98. Do you have any children living at home, of school age or below (i.e.
     dependent)
     . . . . Number

99. Does your wife go out to work?
                Yes—full-time
                Yes—part-time
                No
                Not applicable

100. And where you live, do you
                Rent it—Council
                Rent it—Privately
                Own it—With mortgage
                Own it—Without mortgage
                Pay board and lodging
     INTERVIEWERS COMMENTS

Bibliography

Bendix, R., *Work and Authority in Industry,* (New York, 1963).

Blau, P., and Scott, W.R., *Formal Organisations,* (London, 1963).

Blauner, R., *Alienation and Freedom,* (Chicago, 1964).

Brayfield, Arthur and Crockett, Walter H., 'Employee Attitudes and Employee Performance', *Psychological Bulletin,* Vol. 52, No. 5, (1955).

Brown A., 'Artefacts, Automation and Human Ability' in J.R. Lawrence (ed.)., *Operational Research and the Social Sciences,* (London, 1966).

Brown, R., and Brannen, P., 'Shipbuilding', *Sociology,* Vol. 4., No. 2. (May 1970).

Coleman, J.S., 'Relational Analysis: the study of organisations with survey methods' reprinted in A. Etzioni, *A Sociological Reader in Complex Organisations,* (New York, 1969).

Crossman, E.R.F., 'European Experience with the Changing Nature of Jobs due to Automation', in *The Requirements of Automated Jobs,* (Paris, O.E.C.D., 1965).

Daniel, W.W., 'A Comparative Consideration of Two Industrial Work Groups', *Sociological Review,* Vol. 14., No. 1., (March, 1966).

Dubin, R. Homans, G.C., Mann, F.C. and Miller, D.C., *Leadership and Productivity,* (San Francisco, 1965).

Emery, F.E. and Trist, E.L., 'Socio-Technical Systems' in C.W. Churchman and M. Verhulst (ed.). *Management Science, Models and Techniques,* Vol. 2., (Oxford, 1960).

Etzioni, A., *A Comparative Analysis of Complex Organisations,* (Glencoe, 1961).

Fleishman, E.A., 'Leadership Climate, Human Relations Training and Supervisory Behaviour' in E.A. Fleishman *Studies in Personnel and Industrial Psychology,* (Illinois, 1961).

Fox, Alan., *Industrial Sociology and Industrial Relations.,* Royal Commission on Trade Unions and Employers' Associations, (H.M.S.O., London, 1966).

Goldthorpe, John H., 'Attitudes and Behaviour of Car Assembly Workers: A Deviant Case and a Theoretical Critique', *The British Journal of Sociology,* Vol. XVII, No. 3., (1966).

––, Lockwood, D., Bechhofer, F. and Platt, J., *The Affluent Worker: Industrial Attitudes and Behaviour,* (Cambridge, 1968).
The Affluent Worker in the Class Structure, (Cambridge, 1969).

Gouldner, A.W., 'Organisational Analysis' in R.K. Merton, L. Broom and L.S. Cottrell (eds.) *Sociology Today*, Vol. 2. (New York 1965).

H.M.S.O., *The North-East—a programme for regional development and growth*, London, Cmnd. 2206, (November, 1963).
Sample Census 1966, Economic Activity County Leaflets—Yorkshire North Riding. General Register Office, (London, 1969).

Family Expenditure Survey 1966, (London, 1967).

Ingham, G., *Size of Industrial Organisation and Workers Behaviour*, (Cambridge, 1970).

Kuhn, J.W., *Bargaining in Grievance Settlement*, (New York, 1961).
Kynaston Reeves, T., 'Constrained and Facilitated Behaviour—A Typology of Behaviour in Economic Organisations', *British Journal of Industrial Relations.*, Vol. V. No. 2. (1967).
——,and Turner, Barry A., *A Theory of Organisation and Behaviour in Batch Production Factories*, (Unpublished paper, Imperial College, London, 1970).

Lawrence, Paul and Lorsch, Jay., *Organisation and Environment*, (Boston, 1967).
Lockwood, David., 'Sources of Variation in Working Class Images of Society'., *The Sociological Review*, Vol. 14., No. 3. (1966).

Maslow, A., *Motivation and Personality*, (New York, 1954).

Perrow, C., 'A Framework for the Comparative Analysis of Organisations', *American Sociological Review*, Vol. 32, No. 2. (April, 1967).
Peterson, R.A., 'Must the Quest After Variance End in History?' in M.N. Zald, *Power In Organisations*, (Vanderbilt, 1970).

Rice, A.K., *Productivity and Social Organisation*, (London, 1958).

Sayles, L.R., *The Behaviour of Industrial Work Groups: Prediction and Control*, (New York, 1958).
Schein, E., *Organisational Psychology*, (Englewood Cliffs, 1965).

Turner, A.N. and Lawrence, P., *Industrial Jobs and the Worker*, (Boston, 1965).
Turner, H., Clack, G. and Roberts, G. *Labour Relations in the Motor Industry*, (London, 1967).

Walker, C.R. and Guest, R.H., *The Man on the Assembly Line*, (Cambridge, Mass., 1952).
Wedderburn, Dorothy., 'The Conditions of Employment of Manual and Non-Manual Workers'., *Proceedings of the Social Science Research Council Conference on Social Stratification and Industrial Relations*, (January, 1969).

——, and Craig, J.C., *Relative Deprivation in Work,* Paper read to Section N of the British Association for the Advancement of Science, Exeter, (September, 1969).

Westergaard, J.H., 'The Rediscovery of the Cash Nexus' in R. Miliband and J. Saville, *The Socialist Register,* (London, 1970).

Willener, A., 'Payment Systems in the French Steel and Iron Mining Industry: An Exploration in Managerial Resistance to Change' in G.K. Zollschan and W. Hirsch (ed.) *Explorations in Social Change,* (Boston, 1964).

Woodward, Joan, (ed). *Industrial Organisation: Behaviour and Control,* (Oxford, 1970).

Management and Technology, (H.M.S.O., London, 1958).

Industrial Organisation: Theory and Practice, (London, 1965).

Index

absenteeism, 58, 60–1, 75, 140, 142, 149
age, 92–3, 147
alienation, 18–19, 20
Amalgamated Engineering Union, 29, 101–3
anonymity of site, 38–9
attitudes to the Company, 35–40, 141
automation, 36, 65, 79, 81

behaviour
  constraint evasive, 59–60, 63, 140
  attitudes and, 19, 22, 58–63, 86, 89, 106, 111, 135, 140–2, 145, 146
Bendix, R., 87n
Blau, P., 138n
Blauner, R., 18, 20, 30, 66, 75, 79, 80, 149
bonus, 37, 55, 61, 93, 108, 117, 122, 123–6, 128, 129, 130, 136, 144
Brannen, P., 143n
Brayfield, A. H., 58n, 75n
Brown, A., 65, 67
Brown, R., 143n

chemical process workers, 67–79, 114, 150
  attitudes of, 72–9
  and bonus, 123–4
  and quality control, 126–7
  working conditions, 84
  work task, 80–1
Clack, G., 21n
class consciousness, 144
Coleman, J. S., 134n
contextual analysis, 134
control system (*see also* bonus, quality control,

174

immediate supervision), 24, 25, 86, 116, 121–32, 149
  and social control, 122
  and role of supervision, 129, 138–9
  'craft consciousness', 143–4, 150
craftsmen, *see* tradesmen
Craig, J. C., 15n
Crockett, W. H., 58n, 75n
Crossman, E. R. F., 65

Daniel, W. W., 20n
Dubin, R., 115n, 129n

earnings, *see* 'pay'
economic environment, *see* market situation
Electrical Trades Union, 29, 102, 103
Emery, F. E., 16n
employment history, 90–1, 148
Etzioni, A., 20n

Family Expenditure Survey, 93n
Fleishman, E. A., 115n
formal organisation, 116, 117
Fox, A., 46n

general workers, 29, 31–3, 140, 141
  comparison of attitudes, 57–8
  comparison of Works *A* & *C*, 106–8
  recruitment of, 93, 95
Goldthorpe, J. H., 15n, 22, 23n, 59

Date Due